QUANTUM SCIENCE OF GANESHA CONCIOUSNESS

Prof. (Dr.) Jai Paul Dudeja

ISBN 979-8-88667-597-9

CONTENTS

PREFACE

Dear Readers,

Ganesha consciousness is a state of awareness in which an individual acts in complete harmony with the Divine or the ultimate reality of Ganesha. It is a form of Bhakti yoga (or devotional service) in which the purpose is to devote one's thoughts, actions and worship to pleasing Ganesha, who some consider to be the supreme god. To act with Ganesha consciousness is to free the self from the illusion that it is an individual body. It is a way to experience the bliss of one's true, eternal nature. It is said that anyone can do this and that Ganesha consciousness is something everyone has naturally.

Ganesha Consciousness is the pre-eminent consciousness of all Divine Archetypes. It is beyond time and space, it is capable of the greatest intelligence and wisdom, and is unlimited in its ability to do anything, including: time/space mastery, protection equivalent of Vishnu, wealth equivalent to Lakshmi, purity equal to Shiva, wisdom equal to Murugan (Ganesha's brother), intelligence equal to Saraswati, compassion and power equivalent to Shakti, and mind/body/soul strength equal to Hanuman.

What sets Ganesha apart from all other archetypes is his ability to give results faster. It is because of his special intelligence to remove any obstacles; and bless the devotees with material, mental, emotional, and spiritual benefits.

This book is all about Lord Ganesha, its Consciousness and its correlation with 'Quantum Science'.

This book consists of **9 chapters, divided into the following four sections:**

Section 1: Introduction and Overview (Chapter 1)

Section 2: Lord Ganesha in Hindu Puranas (Chapters 2-6)

Section 3: Ganesha Consciousness (Chapter 7)

Section 4: Science of Ganesha Consciousness (Chapters 8-9).

The **first chapter** is titled, "Lord Ganesha: Introduction and Overview". It is suggested that all the readers must go through this chapter in order to appreciate rest of the book.

Chapters 2-6, discuss the mention of Lord Ganesha in Hindu Puranas, viz., Ganesha Purana, Mudgala Purana, Ganapati Atharvashirsha Purana (Ganapati Upanishad), Skanda Purana, and Shiva Purana, respectively.

Chapter 7 introduces 'Ganesha Consciousness' and describes it in detail.

Chapter 8 discusses the 'Science of Ganesha Consciousness' in fair details.

The last chapter, that is, **Chapter 9,** titled, "Quantum Entanglement and Connection with Ganesha Consciousness" discusses the phenomenon of "Quantum Entanglement" and tries to establish how any individual soul can be merged into the Supreme Soul, that is 'Ganesha Consciousness'.

The author sincerely believes that a book of this nature will be useful for all the readers across the globe who wish to understand the significance of science of Ganesha Consciousness, and get material, mental, emotional, and spiritual benefits from it.

I would gratefully and open heartedly love to receive any encouraging/critical comments as well as feedback from my dear readers at my Email ID: drjpdudeja@gmail.com

Sincerely

Prof. (Dr.) Jai Paul Dudeja
2022

ACKNOWLEDGEMENTS

The seeds of my interest in 'spirituality' were sown more than sixty-five years ago by my revered parents, **Late (Dr.) Shanti Sawrup Dudeja and Late (Mrs.) Jai Devi Dudeja**. I bow to them with gratitude, wherever they are in the other world.

I have greatly benefitted in going through the books and articles referred in the 'Bibliography' in this Book. I gratefully acknowledge these authors for enhancing my understanding on the subject matter of this book.

Last but not the least, my greatest admiration is reserved for **Mrs. Rita Dudeja, my wife**, my best friend, my constant source of inspiration and my co-traveller on the path of truth, for all my ventures and endeavours like this and many others.

Prof. (Dr.) Jai Paul Dudeja
2022

Vakratunda Mahakaya Surya Koti Samaprabha |

Nirvighnam Kuru Me Deva Sarva-Kaaryeshu Sarvadaa ||

"O Lord (Ganesha), who has a huge body, curved elephant trunk and whose brilliance is equal to billions of Suns,

May always remove all obstacles from my endeavours."

SECTION 1:
INTRODUCTION AND OVERVIEW

LORD GANESHA: INTRODUCTION AND OVERVIEW

1.1 Introduction to Lord Ganesha

Each and every Hindu with belief of Dharma, irrespective of caste or gender, wakes off from bed in the morning remembering Ganeshwara to ensure that throughout the following day and night should pass off without obstructions , hurdles or mis-happenings and with contentment, be it from family, surroundings and society, without no shows of evil energies. Ganesha (or Ganesh) is a Hindu god, and the son of Shiva and Parvati. He is the god of wisdom, the lord of good fortune, and is also regarded as the remover of obstacles.

Ganesha is depicted as a short fat man with the head of an elephant. He is one of the most popular and widely worshiped Hindu deities. Worship of Lord Ganesha is thought to bring prosperity, success and protection from evils.

Ganesha (Gaṇeśa), also known as Ganapati and Vinayaka, is one of the best-known and most worshipped deities in the Hinduism. His image is found throughout India, Nepal, Sri Lanka, Thailand, Indonesia (Java and

Bali), Singapore, Malaysia, Philippines, and Bangladesh and in countries with large ethnic Indian populations including Fiji, Guyana, Mauritius, and Trinidad and Tobago. Hindu denominations worship him regardless of affiliations. Devotion to Ganesha is widely diffused and extends to Jains and Buddhists.

Although Ganesha has many attributes, he is readily identified by his elephant head. He is widely revered, more specifically, as the remover of obstacles and thought to bring good luck; the patron of arts and sciences; and the deva of intellect and wisdom. As the god of beginnings, he is honoured at the start of rites and ceremonies. Ganesha is also invoked as a patron of letters and learning during writing sessions. Several texts relate mythological anecdotes associated with his birth and exploits.

An elephant–headed anthropomorphic figure on Indo-Greek coins from the 1st century BCE has been proposed by some scholars to be "incipient Ganesha", while others have suggested Ganesha may have been an emerging deity in India and southeast Asia around the 2nd century CE based on the evidence from archaeological excavations in Mathura and outside India. Most certainly by the 4th and 5th centuries CE, during the Gupta period, Ganesha was well established and had inherited traits from Vedic and pre-Vedic precursors. Hindu mythology identifies him as the restored son of Parvati and Shiva of the Shaivism tradition, but he is a pan-Hindu god found in its various traditions. In the Ganapatya tradition of

Hinduism, Ganesha is the supreme deity. The principal texts on Ganesha include the Ganesha Purana, the Mudgala Purana and the Ganapati Atharvasirsa. Brahma Purana and Brahmanda Purana are other two Puranic genre encyclopaedic texts that deal with Ganesha.

Ganesha has been ascribed many other titles and epithets, including Ganapati (Ganpati), Vighneshvara, and Pillaiyar. The Hindu title of respect Shri (śrī; also spelled Sri or Shree) is often added before his name.

The name Ganesha is a Sanskrit compound, joining the words Gana (gaṇa), meaning a 'group, multitude, or categorical system' and Isha (īśa), meaning 'lord or master'. The word gaṇa when associated with Ganesha is often taken to refer to the ganas, a troop of semi-divine beings that form part of the retinue of Shiva, Ganesha's father. The term more generally means a category, class, community, association, or corporation. Some commentators interpret the name "Lord of the Ganas" to mean "Lord of Hosts" or "Lord of created categories", such as the elements. Ganapati, a synonym for Ganesha, is a compound composed of gaṇa, meaning "group", and pati, meaning "ruler" or "lord". The earliest mention of the word Ganapati is found in hymn 2.23.1 of the 2nd-millennium BCE Rigveda:

Gannaanaam Tvaa Ganna-Patim Havaamahe

Kavim Kaviinaam-Upama-Shravastamam |

Jyessttha-Raajam Brahmannaam Brahmannaspata

Aa Nah Shrnnvan-Uutibhih Siida Saadanam ||

Meaning: Among the Ganas (Group of Prayers), to You Who are the Ganapati (Lord of Prayers), we Offer our Sacrificial Oblations. You are the Wisdom of the Wise and Uppermost in Glory. You are the foremost King of the Prayers, presiding as the Lord of the Prayers (Brahmanaspati). Please come to us by Listening to our Invocation and be Present in the Seat of this Sacred Sacrificial Altar (to charge our Prayers with Your Power and Wisdom).

It is however uncertain that the Vedic term referred above is specifically to Ganesha.

The first two chapters of Sri Ganapati Atharvasirsa declare:

Om Namaste Ganapataye. (1)

Tvameva pratyaksha tattvamasi.

Tvameva krvalam kartaasi.

Tvameva kevalam dhartaasi.

Tvameva kevalam hartaasi.

Tvameva sarvam khalvidam brahmasi.

Tvam sakshadatmaasi nityam. (2)

Meaning: Om, Salutations to You, O Ganapati. (1)

(O Ganapati) You indeed are the visible Tattvam (Conscious Essence underlying everything), (O Ganapati) You indeed are the only Creator (Karta) (by Whose Power the Universe is Created), (O Ganapati) You indeed are the only Sustainer (Dharta) (by Whose Power the Universe is

Sustained), (O Ganapati) You indeed are the only Destroyer (Harta) (by Whose Power the Universe is finally Dissolved in its Conscious Essence), (O Ganapati) You indeed are All This (The Universe), You verily are the Brahman (giving Consciousness to All), (O Ganapati) You are the visible Atman, the Eternal (underlying Reality). (2)

According to Hymn 119, Chapter 6 in Panchadasi, Ganesha came earlier than Lord Shiva:

Puratrayaṁ sādayituṁ vighneśaṁ so'pya pūjayat,
vināyakuṁ prāhu rīśam gāṇapatya mate ratāḥ (119).

Meaning: Even Shiva is not the original creator. This is what the devotees of Ganapati or Ganesha say, because when Lord Shiva had to go to war against the Tripura demons, he worshipped Ganesha first. But for that worship, he would not have succeeded in the victory over Tripuras. Ganesha is always worshipped first, and all the other gods come afterwards. Hence, Ganesha, and not any other being— not Brahma, Vishnu, Shiva—should be regarded as the Supreme Being. This is the opinion of the Ganapati worshippers, according to Panchadasi.

1.2 Iconography of Ganesha

Ganesha is a popular figure in Indian art. Unlike those of some deities, representations of Ganesha show wide variations and distinct patterns changing over time. He may be portrayed standing, dancing, heroically taking action against demons, playing with his family as a boy, or sitting down on an elevated seat, or engaging in a range of contemporary situations.

Ganesha images were prevalent in many parts of India by the 6th century CE. The 13th-century statue pictured is typical of Ganesha statuary from 900 to 1200, after Ganesha had been well-established as an independent deity with his own sect. This example features some of Ganesha's common iconographic elements. A virtually identical statue has been dated between 973 CE and 1200 CE and another similar statue is dated c. 12th century. Ganesha has the head of an elephant and a big belly. This statue has four arms, which is common in depictions of Ganesha. He holds his own broken tusk in his lower-right hand and holds a delicacy, which he samples with his trunk, in his lower-left hand. The motif of Ganesha turning his trunk sharply to his left to taste a sweet in his lower-left hand is a particularly archaic feature. A more primitive statue in one of the Ellora Caves with this general form has been dated to the 7th century. Details of the other hands are difficult to make out on the statue shown. In the standard configuration, Ganesha typically holds an axe or a goad in one upper arm and a pasha (noose) in the other upper arm. In rare instances, he may be depicted with a human head.

The influence of this old constellation of iconographic elements can still be seen in contemporary representations of Ganesha. In one modern form, the only variation from these old elements is that the lower-right hand does not hold the broken tusk but is turned towards the viewer in a gesture of protection or fearlessness (Abhaya mudra). The same combination of four arms and attributes occurs in statues of Ganesha dancing, which is a very popular theme.

1.3 Common Attributes of Ganesha

Ganesha has been represented with the head of an elephant since the early stages of his appearance in Indian art. Puranic myths provide many explanations for how he got his elephant head. One of his popular forms, Heramba-Ganapati, has five elephant heads, and other less-common variations in the number of heads are known. While some texts say that Ganesha was born with an elephant head, he acquires the head later in most stories. The most recurrent motif in these stories is that Ganesha was created by Parvati using clay to protect her and Shiva beheaded him when Ganesha came between Shiva and Parvati. Shiva then replaced Ganesha's original head with that of an elephant. Details of the battle and where the replacement head came to vary from source to source. Another story says that Ganesha was created directly by Shiva's laughter. Because Shiva considered Ganesha too alluring, he gave him the head of an elephant and a protruding belly.

Ganesha's earliest name was Ekadanta (One Tusked), referring to his single whole tusk, the other being broken. Some of the earliest images of Ganesha show him holding his broken tusk. The importance of this distinctive feature is reflected in the Mudgala Purana, which states that the name of Ganesha's second incarnation is Ekadanta. Ganesha's protruding belly appears as a distinctive attribute in his earliest statuary, which dates to the Gupta period (4th to 6th centuries). This feature is so important that according to the Mudgala Purana, two different incarnations of Ganesha use names based on it: Lambodara (Pot Belly, or, literally, Hanging Belly) and Mahodara (Great Belly). Both names are Sanskrit compounds describing his belly (Udara). The Brahmanda Purana says that Ganesha has the name Lambodara because all the universes (i.e., cosmic eggs; brahmāṇḍas) of the past, present, and future are present in him.

The number of Ganesha's arms varies; his best-known forms have between two and sixteen arms. Many depictions of Ganesha feature four arms, which is mentioned in Puranic sources and codified as a standard form in some iconographic texts. His earliest images had two arms. Forms with 14 and 20 arms appeared in Central India during the 9th and the 10th centuries. The serpent is a common feature in Ganesha iconography and appears in many forms. According to the Ganesha Purana, Ganesha wrapped the serpent Vasuki around his neck. Other depictions of snakes include use as a sacred thread (yajñyopavīta) wrapped around the stomach as a belt, held in a hand, coiled at the ankles, or as a throne. Upon Ganesha's forehead may be a third eye or the sectarian mark (tilaka), which consists of three horizontal lines. The Ganesha Purana prescribes a tilaka mark as well as a crescent moon on the forehead. A distinct form of Ganesha called Bhalachandra (bhālacandra; "Moon on the Forehead") includes that iconographic element.

Ganesha is often described as red in colour. Specific colours are associated with certain forms. Many examples of colour associations with specific meditation forms are prescribed in the Sritattvanidhi, a treatise on Hindu iconography. For example, white is associated with his representations as Heramba-Ganapati and Rina-Mochana-Ganapati (Ganapati Who Releases from Bondage). Ekadanta-Ganapati is visualised as blue during meditation in that form.

1.4 Vahanas of Ganesha

The earliest Ganesha images are without a vahana (mount/vehicle). Of the eight incarnations of Ganesha described in the Mudgala Purana, Ganesha uses a mouse (shrew) in five of them, a lion in his incarnation as Vakratunda, a peacock in his incarnation as Vikata, and Shesha, the divine serpent, in his incarnation as Vighnaraja. Mohotkata uses a lion, Mayūreśvara uses a peacock, Dhumraketu uses a horse, and Gajanana uses a mouse, in the four incarnations of Ganesha listed in the Ganesha Purana. Jain depictions of Ganesha show his vahana variously as a mouse, elephant, tortoise, ram, or peacock.

Ganesha is often shown riding on or attended by a mouse, shrew or rat. The rat began to appear as the principal vehicle in sculptures of Ganesha in central and western India during the 7th century; the rat was always placed close to his feet. The mouse as a mount first appears in written sources in the Matsya Purana and later in the Brahmananda Purana and Ganesha Purana, where Ganesha uses it as his vehicle in his last incarnation. The Ganapati Atharvashirsa includes a meditation verse on Ganesha that describes the mouse appearing on his flag. The names Mūṣakavāhana (mouse-mount) and Ākhuketana (rat-banner) appear in the Ganesha Sahasranama.

The mouse is interpreted in several ways. Many, if not most of those who interpret Ganapati's mouse, do so negatively; it symbolizes Tamo guṇa as well as desire. Along these lines. According to another version, it symbolises those who wish to overcome desires and be less selfish. The rat is destructive and a menace to crops. The Sanskrit word mūṣaka (mouse) is derived from the root mūṣ (stealing, robbing). It was essential to subdue the rat as a destructive pest, a type of vighna (impediment) that needed to be overcome. According to this theory, showing Ganesha as master of the rat demonstrates his function as Vigneshvara (Lord of Obstacles) and gives evidence of his possible role as a folk grāma-devatā (village deity) who later rose to greater prominence. A view that the rat is a symbol suggesting that Ganesha, like the rat, penetrates even the most secret places.

1.5 Mythological Anecdotes about Ganesha

1.5.1 How did he obtain his elephant head?

The highly articulated mythology of Hinduism presents many stories which explain how Ganesha obtained his elephant head; often the origin of this particular attribute is to be found in the same anecdotes which tell about his birth. And many of these same stories reveal the origins of the enormous popularity of his cult.

1.5.1.1 Ganesha: Decapitated and Reanimated by Shiva

The most well-known story is probably the one taken from the Shiva Purana. Once, while his mother Parvati wanted to take a bath, there were no attendants around to guard her and stop anyone from accidentally entering the house. One day Goddess Parvati was at home on Mt. Kailash preparing for a bath. As she didn't want to be disturbed, she told Nandi, her husband Shiva's Bull, to guard the door and let no one pass. Nandi faithfully took his post, intending to carry out Parvati's wishes. But, when Shiva came home and naturally wanted to come inside, Nandi had to let him pass, being loyal first to Shiva. Parvati was angry at this slight, but even more than this, at the fact that she had no one as loyal to Herself as Nandi was to Shiva.

Hence she created an image of a boy out of turmeric paste which she prepared to cleanse her body (turmeric was used for its antiseptic and cooling properties), and infused life into it, and thus Ganesha was born. Parvati ordered Ganesha not to allow anyone to enter the house, and Ganesha obediently followed his mother's orders. In due course, Shiva came home, only to find this strange boy telling him that he couldn't enter his own house! He told Ganesha that he was Parvati's husband, and demanded that Ganesha let him go in. But Ganesha would not hear any person's word other than his dear mother's. Shiva lost his patience and had a fierce battle with Ganesha. At last he severed Ganesha's head with his Trishula (trident). When Parvati came out and saw her son's lifeless body, she was very angry and sad. She demanded that Shiva restore Ganesha's life at once.

Unfortunately, Shiva's Trishula was so powerful that it had hurled Ganesha's head very far off. All attempts to find the head were in vain. As a last resort, Shiva approached Brahma who suggested that he replace Ganesha's head with the first living being that came his way which lay with its head facing north. Shiva then sent his celestial armies (Gana) to find and take the head of whatever creature they happened to find asleep with its head facing north. They found a dying elephant which slept in this manner, and after its death took its head, attaching the elephant's head to Ganesha's body and bringing him back to life. From then on, he was called Ganapathi, or head of the celestial armies, and was to be worshipped by everyone before beginning any activity.

1.5.1.2 Shiva and Gajasura

Another story regarding the origins of Ganesha and his elephant head narrates that, once, there existed an Asura (demon) with all the characteristics of an elephant, called Gajasura, who was undergoing a penitence (or tapas). Shiva, satisfied by this austerity, decided to grant him, as a reward, whatever gift he desired. The demon wished that he could emanate fire continually from his own body so that no one could ever dare to approach him. The Lord granted him his request. Gajasura continued his penitence and Shiva, who appeared in front of him from time to time, asked him once again what he desired. The demon responded: "I desire that You inhabit my stomach."

Shiva granted even this request and he took up residence in the demon's stomach. In fact, Shiva is also known as Bhola (innocent) Shankara because he is a deity easily propitiated; when he is satisfied with a devotee he grants him whatever he desires, and this, from time to time, generates particularly intricate situations. It was for this reason that Parvati, his wife, sought him everywhere without results. As a last recourse, she went to her brother Vishnu, asking him to find her husband. He, who knows everything, reassured her: "Don't worry, dear sister, your husband is Bhola Shankara and promptly grants to his devotees whatever they ask of him, without regard for the consequences; for this reason, I think he has gotten himself into some trouble. I will find out what has happened."

Then Vishnu, the omniscient director of the cosmic game, staged a small comedy. He transformed Nandi (the bull of Shiva) into a dancing bull and conducted him in front of Gajasura, assuming, at the same time, the appearance of a flutist. The enchanting performance of the bull sent the demon into ecstasies, and he asked the flutist to tell him what he desired. The musical Vishnu responded: "Can you give me that which I ask?" Gajasura replied: "Who do you take me for? I can immediately give you whatever you ask." The flutist then said: "If that's so, liberate Shiva from your stomach." Gajasura understood then that this must have been no other than Vishnu himself, the only one who could have known that secret and he threw himself at his feet. Having liberated Shiva, he asked him for one last gift: "I have been blessed by you with many gifts; my last request is that everyone remember me adoring my head when I am dead." Shiva then brought his own son there and replaced his head with that of Gajasura. From then on, in India, the tradition is that any action, in order to prosper, one must begin with the adoration of Ganesha. This is the result of the gift of Shiva to Gajasura.

1.5.1.3 The gaze of Shani

A less well-known story from the Brahma Vaivarta Purana narrates a different version of Ganesha's birth. On the insistence of Shiva, Parvati fasted for a year (punyaka vrata) to propitiate Vishnu so that he would grant her a son. Lord Vishnu, after the completion of the sacrifice, announced that he would incarnate himself as her son in every kalpa (eon). Accordingly, Krishna was born to Parvati as a charming infant. This event was celebrated with great enthusiasm and all the gods were invited to take a look at the baby. However Shani (Saturn), the son of Surya, hesitated to look at the baby since Shani was cursed with the gaze of destruction. However Parvati insisted that he look at the baby, which Shani did, and immediately the infant's head fell off and flew to Goloka. Seeing Shiva and Parvati grief stricken, Vishnu mounted on Garuda, his divine eagle, and rushed to the banks of the Pushpa-Bhadra river, from where he brought back the head of a young elephant. The head of the elephant was joined with the headless body of Parvati's son, thus reviving him. The infant was named Ganesha and all the Gods blessed Ganesha and wished Him power and prosperity.

1.5.1.4 Curse of Kashyap

Another tale of Ganesha's birth relates to an incident in which Shiva slew Aditya, the son of a sage. Shiva restored life to the dead boy, but this could not pacify the outraged sage Kashyapa, who was one of the seven great Rishis. Kashyap cursed Shiva and declared that Shiva's son would lose his head. When this happened, the head of Indra's elephant was used to replace it.

1.5.1.5 Birth the Elephant-headed Goddess Malini

Still another tale states that on one occasion, Parvati's used bath-water was thrown into the Ganges, and this water was drunk by the elephant-headed Goddess Malini, who gave birth to a baby with four arms and five elephant heads. The river goddess Ganga claimed him as her son, but Shiva declared him to be Parvati's son, reduced his five heads to one and enthroned him as the Controller of obstacles (Vigneshvara).

1.6 How did Ganesha's tusk break off?

There are various anecdotes which explain how Ganesha broke off one of his tusks.

1.6.1 Ganesha the Scribe

In the first part of the epic poem Mahabharata, it is written that the sage Vyasa asked Ganesha to transcribe the poem as he dictated it to him. Ganesha agreed, but only on the condition that Vyasa recite the poem uninterruptedly, without pausing. The sage, in his turn, posed the condition that Ganesha would not only have to write, but would have to understand everything that he heard before writing it down. In this way, Vyasa might recuperate a bit from his continuous talking by simply reciting a difficult verse which Ganesha could not understand. The dictation began, but in the rush of writing, Ganesha's feather pen broke. He broke off a tusk and used it as a pen so that the transcription could proceed without interruption, permitting him to keep his word.

1.6.2 Ganesha and Parashurama

One day Parashurama, an avatar of Vishnu, went to pay a visit to Shiva, but along the way he was blocked by Ganesha. Parashurama hurled his axe at Ganesha and Ganesha (knowing that this axe was given to him by Shiva) allowed himself out of respect to be struck and lost his tusk as a result.

1.6.3 Ganesha and the Moon

It is said that one day Ganesha, after having received amounts of sweets (Modak) from many of his devotees an enormous, in order to better digest this incredible mass of food, decided to go for a ride. He got on the mouse which he used as his vehicle and took off. It was a magnificent night and the moon was resplendent. Suddenly a snake appeared out of nowhere and nearly frightened the mouse to death, causing it to jump and Ganesha was thrown off his mount. Ganesha's huge stomach smashed against the ground so forcefully that it burst open and all of the sweets that he had eaten were scattered around him. Nonetheless, he was too intelligent to get angry about this accident and, without wasting any time in useless lamentations, he tried to remedy the situation as best he could. He took the serpent which had caused the accident and used it as a belt to keep his stomach closed and bandage the injury. Satisfied by this solution, he remounted his mouse and continued his excursion. Chandra dev (Moon God) saw the whole scene and laughed. Ganesha, being the short-tempered one, cursed Chandra dev for his arrogance and breaking off one of his tusks, hurled it against the Moon, slashing its luminous face in two. He then cursed it, decreeing that anyone who happens to see the moon will incur bad luck. Hearing this, Chandra dev realized his folly and asked for forgiveness from Ganesha. Ganesha relented and since a curse cannot be revoked, only softened it. Ganesha softened his curse such that the moon would wax and wane in intensity every fifteen days and anyone who looks at the moon during Ganesh Chaturthi would incur bad-luck. This explains why, in certain moments, the light of the Moon goes off and then begins gradually to reappear; but its face appears whole only for a brief period of time, since it is once again "broken" in half to the point of disappearing.

1.7 Ganesha, the Head of Celestial Armies

There once took place a great competition between the Devas to decide who among them should be the head of the Gana (the troops of semi-gods at the service of Shiva). The competitors were required to circle the world as fast as possible and return to the Feet of Shiva. The gods took off, each on his or her own vehicle, and even Ganesha participated with enthusiasm in the race; but he was extremely heavy and was riding on a mouse! Naturally, his pace was remarkably slow and this was a great disadvantage. He had not yet made much headway when there appeared before him the sage Narada (son of Brahma), who asked him where he was going. Ganesha was very annoyed and went into a rage because it was considered unlucky to encounter a solitary Brahmin just at the beginning of a voyage. Notwithstanding the fact that Narada was the greatest of Brahmins, son of Brahma himself, this was still a bad omen. Moreover, it wasn't considered a good sign to be asked where one was heading when one was already on the way to some destination; therefore, Ganesha felt doubly unfortunate.

Nonetheless, the great Brahmin succeeded in calming his fury. Ganesha explained to him the motives for his sadness and his terrible desire to win. Narada consoled and exhorted him not to despair.

Ganesha returned to his father, who asked him how he was able to finish the race so quickly. Ganesha told him of his encounter with Narada and of the Brahmin's counsel. Shiva, satisfied with this response, pronounced his son the winner and, from that moment on, he was acclaimed with the name of Ganapati (Conductor of the celestial armies) and Vinayaka (Lord of all beings).

1.8 Ganesha's Appetite

One anecdote, taken from the Purana, narrates that the treasurer of Svarga (paradise) and god of wealth, Kubera, went one day to Mount Kailasha in order to receive the darshan (vision) of Shiva. Since he was extremely vain, he invited Shiva to a feast in his fabulous city, Alakapuri, so that he could show off to him all of his wealth. Shiva smiled and said to him: "I cannot come, but you can invite my son Ganesha. But I warn you that he is a voracious eater." Unperturbed, Kubera felt confident that he could satisfy even the most insatiable appetite, like that of Ganesha, with his opulence. He took the little son of Shiva with him into his great city. There, he offered him a ceremonial bath and dressed him in sumptuous clothing. After these initial rites, the great banquet began. While the servants of Kubera were working themselves to the bone in order to bring the portions, the little Ganesha just continued to eat and eat and eat.... His appetite did not decrease even after he had devoured the servings which were destined for the other guests. There was not even any time to substitute one plate with another because Ganesha had already devoured everything, and with gestures of impatience, continued waiting for more food. Having devoured everything which had been prepared, Ganesha began eating the decorations, the tableware, the furniture, the chandelier.... Terrified, Kubera prostrated himself in front of the little omnivorous one and requested him to spare him, at least, the rest of the palace.

"I am hungry. If you don't give me something else to eat, I will eat you as well!", he said to Kubera. Desperate, Kubera rushed to mount Kailasha to ask Shiva to remedy the situation. The Lord then gave him a handful of roasted rice, saying that something as simple as a handful of roasted rice would satiate Ganesha, if it was offered with humility and love. Ganesha had swallowed up almost the entire city when Kubera finally arrived and humbly gave him the rice. With that, Ganesha was finally satisfied and calmed.

1.9 Ganesha's Reverence for his Parents

Once there was a competition between Ganesha and his brother Murugan as to who could circumambulate the three worlds faster and hence win the fruit of knowledge. Murugan went off on a journey to cover the three worlds while Ganesha simply circumambulated his parents. When asked why he did so, he answered that his parents

Shiva and Parvati constituted the three worlds, and was given the fruit of knowledge.

1.10 Devotion of Ganesha to his Mother

While playing, once, Ganesha wounded a cat. When he returned home he found a wound in his Mother's body. He enquired how she got hurt. Mother Parvati replied that this was caused by none other than Ganesha himself ! Surprised, Ganesha wanted to know when he hurt her. Parvati explained that She as Divine Power was immanent in all beings. When he wounded the cat she was hurt. Ganesha realized that all women were veritable manifestations of his Mother. He decided not to marry. That's how he remained a Brahmachari, a life-long celibate, following the strict rules of Brahmacharya. However, in some scriptures and images Ganesha is often portrayed as married to the two daughters of Brahma: Riddhi (Knowledge) and Siddhi (Perfection).

1.11 Was Ganesha Married or Celibate?

It is interesting to note how, according to tradition, Ganesha was generated by his mother Parvati without the intervention of her husband Shiva. Shiva, in fact, being eternal (Sadashiva), did not feel any need to have children. Consequently, the relationship of Ganesha and his mother is unique and special.

This devotion is the reason that the traditions of southern India represent him as celibate. It is said that Ganesha, believing his mother to be the most beautiful and perfect woman in the universe, exclaimed: "Bring me a woman as beautiful as she and I will marry her."

In the north of India, on the other hand, Ganesha is often portrayed as married to the two daughters of Brahma: Riddhi (intellect) and Siddhi (spiritual power). On Diwali, he is combined with Lakshmi (goddess of luck and prosperity), and Sarasvati (goddess of culture and art) who reflect these two forces. Ganesha is dear to all the Goddesses. Symbolically this represents the fact that wealth, prosperity and success accompany those who have the qualities wisdom, prudence, patience, etc. that Ganesha symbolizes.

There is another mythology, especially in Bengal, which goes in that Ganesha is married to the Kalabou. The Kalabou is nothing but a banana tree draped in traditional white with a Bengali saree with a red border. The story goes that, when Ganesha was supposed to marry, one day when he came home, he saw his mother Durga eating with all her ten hands. Shocked, he asked why is she doing it. Durga replied that if, after Ganesha marries, his wife would not give Durga any food, so Durga is eating to her heart's content with all ten hands. Feeling very sad, Ganesha decided that he would marry a banana tree or Kalabou so that her mother never has any worries about food, as a banana tree cannot stop her from eating.

In the early hours of Saptami, the kalabou is taken for a bath to the Holy Ganges. Water from the Ganges accompanied with Dhak and Kanshi finishes the bathing ceremony. After the bathing ceremony she is adorned in a red-bordered white sari and vermilion is smeared on its leaves. She is then placed on a decorated pedestal and worshipped with flowers, sandalwood paste, and incense sticks. Later she is placed on the right side of Lord Ganesh. This is the reason she is popularly known as Ganesh's wife.

1.12 Significance of Mystical Facts about Lord Ganesha

The ancient rishis were so deeply intelligent that they chose to express Divinity in terms of symbols rather than words, since words change over time, but symbols remain unchanged. When we worship Lord Ganesha the qualities that he represent gets kindled within us.

(i) **Gana:** Signifies the ultimate truth that this existing world is nothing but a collection of molecules. This is called as 'Gana' (collective form). Our own body is a 'Gana'. It is made up of flesh, blood and bone marrow. Thus the Lord of all 'Ganas' is 'GANESHA'.

(ii) **Elephant-head:** Signifies authority, endurance, strength and courage. The elephant head indicates fidelity, intelligence and discriminative power;

(iii) **Mouse as a vehicle**: Signifies the mouse nibbling away at ropes that bind. Just like a mantra which can cut through sheets and sheets of ignorance and carry even an elephant through.

(iv) **Big Belly:** Signifies generosity and total acceptance. Ganesha's pot belly contains infinite universes. It signifies the bounty of nature and equanimity, the ability of Ganesha to swallow the sorrows of the Universe and protect the world.

(v) **Single tusk:** Signifies one-pointedness. The fact that he has a single tusk (the other being broken off) indicates Ganesha's ability to overcome all forms of dualism.

(vi) **Four Arms:** The four arms of Ganesha represent the four inner attributes of the subtle body, that is: mind (Manas), intellect (Buddhi), ego (Ahamkara), and conditioned conscience (Chitta). Lord Ganesha represents the pure consciousness - the Atman - which enables these four attributes to function in us.

(vii) **Hand weaving an Axe:** The hand waving an axe, is a symbol of the retrenchment of all desires, bearers of pain and suffering. With this axe Ganesha can both strike and repel obstacles. The axe is also to prod man to the path of righteousness and truth;

(viii) **Hand holding a Whip:** The second hand holds a whip, symbol of the force that ties the devout person to the eternal beatitude of God. The whip conveys that worldly attachments and desires should be rid of.

(ix) **Lowered hand :** The third hand, turned towards the devotee, is in a pose of blessing, refuge and protection (abhaya). It signifies endless giving and also symbolizes the fact that we will all dissolve into the earth one day.

(x) **Hand holding the Lotus Flower:** The fourth hand holds a lotus flower (Padma), and it symbolizes the highest goal of human evolution, the sweetness of the realized inner self.

(xi) **Riddhi & Siddhi wives of Lord Ganesha:** Signifies that both Riddhi (intelligence) and Siddhi (enhanced abilities) go together with wisdom. Lord Ganesha is considered to be the Lord of Wisdom.

(xii) **Ankusha and noose:** The Ankusha (the goad/ stick that is used to prod an elephant awake) signifies 'awakening' and the 'Paasa' (the noose) which signifies control. Together they signify that with inner-awakening, a lot of energy is released which can go haywire without proper guidance (control).

(xiii) **The wide ears:** These denote wisdom, ability to listen to people who seek help and to reflect on spiritual truths. They signify the importance of listening in order to assimilate ideas. Ears are used to gain knowledge. The large ears indicate that when God is known, all knowledge is known.

(xiv) **Curved Trunk:** The curved trunk indicates the intellectual potentialities which manifest themselves in the faculty of discrimination between real and unreal.

(xv) **Tilaka on the Forehead:** On the forehead, the Trishula (weapon of Shiva, similar to Trident) is depicted, symbolizing time (past, present and future) and Ganesha's mastery over it.

(xvi) **Position of Legs:** The position of his legs (one resting on the ground and one raised) indicate the importance of living and participating in the material world as well as in the spiritual world, the ability to live in the world without being of the world.

(xvii) **Modak:** The 'Modak' in Ganesha's hand is the attainment of the 'Ultimate Bliss'.

1.13 Attributes of Lord Ganesha

1.13.1 Removal of obstacles

Ganesha is Vighneshvara (Vighnaraja, Vighnaharta), the Lord of Obstacles, both of a material and spiritual order. He is popularly worshipped as a remover of obstacles, though traditionally he also places obstacles in the path of those who need to be checked. Hence, he is often worshipped by the people before they begin anything new. Ganesha's dharma and his raison d'être is to create and remove obstacles.

Some of Ganesha's names reflect shadings of multiple roles that have evolved over time. The quick ascension of Ganesha in the Hindu pantheon, and the emergence of the Ganapatyas, to this shift in emphasis from vighnakartā (obstacle-creator) to vighnahartā (obstacle-averter). However, both functions continue to be vital to his character.

1.13.2 Buddhi (Intelligence)

Ganesha is considered to be the Lord of letters and learning. In Sanskrit, the word buddhi is an active noun that is variously translated as intelligence, wisdom, or intellect. The concept of buddhi is closely associated with the personality of Ganesha, especially in the Puranic period, when many stories stress his cleverness and love of intelligence. One of Ganesha's names in the Ganesha Purana and the Ganesha Sahasranama is Buddhipriya. This name also appears in a list of 21 names in the Ganesha Sahasranama that Ganesha says are especially important. The word priya can mean "fond of", and in a marital context it can mean "lover" or "husband", so the name may mean either "Fond of Intelligence" or "Buddhi's Husband".

1.13.3 Om

Ganesha is identified with the Hindu mantra Om. The term oṃkārasvarūpa (Om is his form), when identified with Ganesha, refers to the notion that he personifies the primal sound. The Ganapati Atharvashirsa attests to this association. The relevant passage is translated as follows:

(O Lord Ganapati!) You are (the Trimurti) Brahma, Vishnu, and Mahesa. You are Indra. You are fire [Agni] and air [Vāyu]. You are the sun [Sūrya] and the moon [Chandrama]. You are Brahman. You are (the three worlds) Bhuloka [earth], Antariksha-loka [space], and Swargaloka [heaven]. You are Om. (That is to say, You are all this).

Some devotees see similarities between the shape of Ganesha's body in iconography and the shape of Om in the Devanāgarī and Tamil scripts.

1.13.4 First Chakra

According to Kundalini yoga, Ganesha resides in the first chakra, called Muladhara (mūlādhāra). Mula means "original, main"; adhara means "base, foundation". The muladhara chakra is the principle on which the manifestation or outward expansion of primordial Divine Force rests. This association is also attested to in the Ganapati Atharvashirsa. This passage is translated as follows: "You continually dwell in the sacral plexus at the base of the spine [mūlādhāra cakra]." Thus, Ganesha has a permanent abode in every being at the Muladhara. Ganesha holds, supports and guides all other chakras, thereby "governing the forces that propel the wheel of life".

1.14 Family and Consorts of Ganesha

Though Ganesha is popularly held to be the son of Shiva and Parvati, the Puranic myths give different versions about his birth. In some he was created by Parvati, or by Shiva or created by Shiva and Parvati; in another he appeared mysteriously and was discovered by Shiva and Parvati or he was born from the elephant headed goddess Malini after she drank Parvati's bath water that had been thrown in the river.

The family includes his brother, the god of war, Kartikeya, who is also called Skanda and Murugan. Regional differences dictate the order of their births. In northern India, Skanda is generally said to be the elder, while in the south, Ganesha is considered the first-born. In northern India, Skanda was an important martial deity from about 500 BCE to about 600 CE, after which worship of him declined significantly. As Skanda fell, Ganesha rose. Several stories tell of sibling rivalry between the brothers and may reflect sectarian tensions.

Ganesha's marital status, the subject of considerable scholarly review, varies widely in mythological stories. One pattern of myths identifies Ganesha as an unmarried brahmachari. This view is common in southern India and parts of northern India. Another popularly-accepted mainstream pattern associates him with the concepts of Buddhi (intellect), Siddhi (spiritual power), and Riddhi (prosperity); these qualities are personified as goddesses, said to be Ganesha's wives. He also may be shown with a single consort or a nameless servant (daṣi). Another pattern connects Ganesha with the goddess of culture and the arts, Sarasvati or Śarda (particularly in

Maharashtra). He is also associated with the goddess of luck and prosperity, Lakshmi. Another pattern, mainly prevalent in the Bengal region, links Ganesha with the banana tree, Kala Bo.

The Shiva Purana says that Ganesha had begotten two sons: Kṣema (safety) and Lābha (profit). In northern Indian variants of this story, the sons are often said to be Śubha (auspiciousness) and Lābha. The 1975 Hindi film Jai Santoshi Maa shows Ganesha married to Riddhi and Siddhi and having a daughter named Santoshi Ma, the goddess of satisfaction. This story has no Puranic basis.

1.15 Ganesha's Worship and Festivals

Ganesha is worshipped on many religious and secular occasions, especially at the beginning of ventures such as buying a vehicle or starting a business. There can hardly be a [Hindu] home [in India] which does not house an idol of Ganapati.... Ganapati, being the most popular deity in India, is worshipped by almost all castes and in all parts of the country. Devotees believe that if Ganesha is propitiated, he grants success, prosperity and protection against adversity, etc.

Ganesha is a non-sectarian deity. Hindus of all denominations invoke him at the beginning of prayers, important undertakings, and religious ceremonies. Dancers and musicians, particularly in southern India, begin art performances such as the Bharatnatyam dance with a prayer to Ganesha. Mantras such as **Om Shri**

Ganeshāya Namah (Om, salutation to the Illustrious Ganesha) are often used. One of the most famous mantras associated with Ganesha is *Om Gaṃ Ganapataye Namah* (Om, Gaṃ, Salutation to the Lord of Hosts).

Devotees offer Ganesha sweets such as modaka, small sweet balls called laddus. He is often shown carrying a bowl of sweets, called a modakapātra. Because of his identification with the colour red, he is often worshipped with red sandalwood paste (raktachandana) or red flowers. Dūrvā grass (Cynodon dactylon) and other materials are also used in his worship.

Festivals associated with Ganesh are Ganesh Chaturthi or Vināyaka Chaturthi in the śuklapakṣa (the fourth day of the waxing moon) in the month of Bhadrapada (August/September) and the Ganesh Jayanti (Ganesha's birthday) celebrated on the cathurthī of the śuklapakṣa (fourth day of the waxing moon) in the month of magha (January/February)."

1.15.1 Ganesha Chaturthi

Ganesh Chaturthi is a 10-day long Hindu festival, celebrated throughout India. The festival is held every year in the Hindu month of Bhadra, which falls between mid-August and mid-September. Ganesh Chaturthi honours the birth of Ganesha, the elephant-headed Hindu God, believed to be the remover of obstacles.

It is a public festival, in which local communities compete with one another to showcase the most impressive Ganesha statue and display. The festival begins with people bringing in clay idols of Ganesha, symbolising the god's visit. On the final day of the festival, Ananta Chaturdashi, the Ganesha statues are paraded through the streets. During the parade, people gather to sing and dance, and the Ganesha statue is usually immersed in a body of water such as the ocean or a river. When Ganesha is underwater, it is believed that his presence leaves the statue and returns to Parvati and Shiva. Some families have a tradition of immersion on the 2nd, 3rd, 5th, or 7th day.

Although Ganesh Chaturthi is widely celebrated throughout India, the main celebrations take place in Pune, a city in Maharashtra state in which the festival originated more than 125 years ago. Elaborately decorated statues of the Elephant God are installed in homes, towns and cities throughout Ganesh Chaturthi. A ceremony known as Pranapratishhtha Puja is performed to invoke the presence of Ganesha within the statues. This ritual involves mantra chanting, offerings and prayers to the God.

In 1893, Lokmanya Tilak transformed this annual Ganesha festival from private family celebrations into a grand public event. He did so "to bridge the gap between the Brahmins and the non-Brahmins and find an appropriate context in which to build a new grassroots unity between them" in his nationalistic strivings against the British in Maharashtra. Because of Ganesha's wide appeal as "the god for Everyman", Tilak chose him as a rallying point for Indian protest against British rule. Tilak was the first to install large public images of Ganesha in pavilions, and he established the practice of submerging all the public images on the tenth day. Today, Hindus across India celebrate the Ganapati festival with great fervour, though it is most popular in the state of Maharashtra. The festival also assumes huge proportions in Mumbai, Pune, and in the surrounding belt of Ashtavinayaka temples.

In recent times, Ganesha idols are being made out of Plaster of Paris instead of mud and cause pollution when immersed in rivers and lakes. The idea of rituals like this is to honour the Divinity around us, in our environment, not to cause pollution. Pooja does not mean just lighting a lamp or dumping things into the river. Real puja is feeling a sense of responsibility and belongingness towards nature and creation.

The best way to make a Ganesha idol would be out of a guava-sized ball of turmeric. According to one version of the story of Ganesha's birth, Parvati created the idol of a boy out of turmeric paste before bringing him to life and installing him as her gatekeeper. Another way to make Ganesha could be out of cow dung. Gobar Ganesh is still made in many villages and considered very auspicious. Alternatively, the idol could also be made out of clay. Natural ingredients and colours like kumkum, flour and sandalwood paste can be used to decorate Ganesha. Not only is this better for the environment, when you make the idol yourself, you feel a much deeper connection with Ganesha. The idol-making activity could be done together by the whole family like a project which will promote bonding and also bring out creativity. At the end of the festival, the idol could be immersed in a bucket of water at home which could later be used for plants.

The ritual of immersing (visarjan) the idols after few days of worship reinforces the understanding that God is not in the idol, He is inside us. So experiencing the Omnipresent in the form and deriving joy out of the form is the essence of the Ganesh Chaturthi festival. In a way, such organized festivity and worships lead to an upsurge in enthusiasm and devotion.

Ganesha is the lord of all the good qualities in us. He is also the Lord of knowledge and wisdom. Knowledge dawns only when we become aware of the Self. When there is inertia, there is no knowledge, no wisdom, nor is there any liveliness or progress in life. So the consciousness has to be awakened and the presiding deity of consciousness is Ganesha. That's why before every puja, 'Lord Ganesha is worshipped to awaken the consciousness.

Therefore, install the idol, worship it with infinite love, meditate and experience Lord Ganesha from within. This is the symbolic essence of Ganesh Chaturthi festival, to awaken the Ganesh tattva which is masked inside us.

1.16 Ganesha's Temples

In Hindu temples, Ganesha is depicted in various ways: as a subordinate deity (pārśva-devatā); as a deity related to the principal deity (parivāra-devatā); or as the principal deity of the temple (pradhāna). As the god of transitions, he is placed at the doorway of many Hindu temples to keep out the unworthy, which is analogous to his role as Parvati's doorkeeper. In addition, several shrines are dedicated to Ganesha himself, of which the Ashtavinayaka (aṣṭavināyaka; lit. "eight Ganesha (shrines)") in Maharashtra are particularly well known. Located within a 100-kilometer radius of the city of Pune, each of the eight shrines celebrates a particular form of Ganapati, complete with its own lore. The eight shrines are: Morgaon, Siddhatek, Pali, Mahad, Theur, Lenyadri, Ozar and Ranjangaon.

There are many other important Ganesha temples at the following locations: Wai in Maharashtra; Ujjain in Madhya Pradesh; Jodhpur, Nagaur and Raipur (Pali) in Rajasthan; Baidyanath in Bihar; Baroda, Dholaka, and Valsad in Gujarat and Dhundiraj Temple in Varanasi, Uttar Pradesh. Prominent Ganesha temples in southern India include the following: Kanipakam in Andhra Pradesh; the Rockfort Ucchi Pillayar Temple at Tiruchirapalli in Tamil Nadu; Kottarakkara, Pazhavangadi, Kasargod in Kerala; Hampi, and Idagunji in Karnataka; and Bhadrachalam in Telangana.

Every village however small has its own image of Vighneśvara (Vigneshvara) with or without a temple to house it in. At entrances of villages and forts, below pīpaḷa (Sacred fig) trees... in a niche... in temples of Viṣṇu (Vishnu) as well as Śiva (Shiva) and also in separate shrines specially constructed in Śiva temples... the figure of Vighneśvara is invariably seen. Ganesha temples have also been built outside of India, including Southeast Asia, Nepal (including the four Vinayaka shrines in the Kathmandu Valley), and in several western countries.

1.17 Rise of Ganesha to Prominence

1.17.1 First Appearance

First terracotta images of Ganesha are from 1st century CE found in Ter, Pal, Verrapuram, and Chandraketugarh. These figures are small, with an elephant head, two arms, and chubby physique. The earliest Ganesha icons in stone were carved in Mathura during Kushan times (2nd–3rd centuries CE).

Ganesha appeared in his classic form as a clearly-recognizable deity with well-defined iconographic attributes in the early 4th to 5th centuries CE. Some of the earliest known Ganesha images include two images found in eastern Afghanistan. The first image was discovered in the ruins north of Kabul along with those of Surya and Shiva. It is dated to the 4th-century. The second image found in Gardez, the Gardez Ganesha, has an inscription on Ganesha pedestal that has helped date it to the 5th-century. Another Ganesha sculpture is embedded in the walls of Cave 6 of the Udayagiri Caves in Madhya Pradesh. This is dated to the 5th-century. An early iconic image of Ganesha with elephant head, a bowl of sweets and a goddess sitting in his lap has been found in the ruins of the Bhumara Temple in Madhya Pradesh, and this is dated to the 5th-century Gupta period. Other recent discoveries, such as the one from Ramgarh Hill, are also dated to the 4th or 5th centuries. An independent cult with Ganesha as the primary deity was well established by about the 10th century.

The evidence for more ancient Ganesha, may reside outside Brahmanic or Sanskritic traditions, or outside geo-cultural boundaries of India. Ganesha appears in China by the 6th century, states Brown, and his artistic images in temple setting as "remover of obstacles" in South Asia appear by about 400 CE. He is recognised as goddess Parvati's son and integrated into Shaivism theology by early centuries of the common era.

1.17.2 Vedic and Epic Literature

The title "Leader of the group" (gaṇapati) occurs twice in the Rig Veda, but in neither case does it refer to the modern Ganesha. The term appears in RV 2.23.1 (described earlier) as a title for Brahmanaspati, according to commentators. While this verse doubtless refers to Brahmanaspati, it was later adopted for worship of Ganesha and is still used today. In rejecting any claim that this passage is evidence of Ganesha in the Rig Veda, it is said that it "clearly refers to Bṛhaspati—who is the deity of the hymn—and Bṛhaspati only". Equally clearly, the second passage (RV 10.112.9) refers to Indra, who is given the epithet 'gaṇapati', translated "Lord of the companies (of the Maruts)." However, it is noted that the more recent Ganapatya literature often quotes the Rigvedic verses to give Vedic respectability to Ganesha.

The Sangam period Tamil poet Avvaiyar (3rd century BCE), invokes Ganesha while preparing the invitation to the three Tamil Kingdoms for giving away in marriage of Angavay and Sangavay of Ceylon in marriage to the King of Tirucovalur (pp. 57–59).

Two verses in texts belonging to Black Yajurveda, Maitrāyaṇīya Saṃhitā (2.9.1) and Taittirīya Āraṇyaka (10.1), appeal to a deity as "the tusked one" (Dantiḥ), "elephant-faced" (Hastimukha), and "with a curved trunk" (Vakratuṇḍa). These names are suggestive of Ganesha, and the 14th century commentator Sayana explicitly establishes this identification. The description of Dantin, possessing a twisted trunk (vakratuṇḍa) and holding a corn-sheaf, a sugar cane, and a club, is so characteristic of the Puranic Ganapati that we cannot resist to accept his full identification with this Vedic Dantin. However, these hymns could be post-Vedic additions. These passages are generally considered to have been interpolated. The references to the elephant-headed deity in the Maitrāyaṇī Saṃhitā have been proven to be very late interpolations, and thus are not very helpful for determining the early formation of the deity.

Ganesha does not appear in the Indian epic literature that is dated to the Vedic period. A late interpolation to the epic poem Mahabharata (1.1.75–79) says that the sage Vyasa (Vyāsa) asked Ganesha to serve as his scribe to transcribe the poem as he dictated it to him. Ganesha agreed but only on the condition that Vyasa recites the poem uninterrupted, that is, without pausing. The sage agreed but found that to get any rest he needed to recite very complex passages so Ganesha would have to ask for clarifications. The story is not accepted as part of the original text by the editors of the critical edition of the Mahabharata, in which the twenty-line story is relegated to a footnote in an appendix. The story of Ganesha acting as the scribe occurs in 37 of the 59 manuscripts consulted during the preparation of the critical edition. Ganesha's association with mental agility and learning is one reason he is shown as scribe for Vyāsa's dictation of the Mahabharata in this interpolation. The term vināyaka is found in some recensions of the Śāntiparva and Anuśāsanaparva that are regarded as interpolations. A reference to Vighnakartṛīṇām ("Creator of Obstacles") in Vanaparva is also believed to be an interpolation and does not appear in the critical edition.

1.17.3 Puranic period

Stories about Ganesha often occur in the Puranic corpus. While the Puranas defy precise chronological ordering, the more detailed narratives of Ganesha's life are in the late texts, c. 600–1300. The Puranic myths about the birth of Ganesha and how he acquired an elephant's head are in the later Puranas, which were composed of c. 600 onwards. It is elaborated that references to Ganesha in the earlier Puranas, such as the Vayu and Brahmanda

Puranas, are later interpolations made during the 7th to 10th centuries.

One cannot help being struck by the fact that the numerous stories surrounding Gaṇeśa concentrate on an unexpectedly limited number of incidents. These incidents are mainly three: his birth and parenthood, his elephant head, and his single tusk. Other incidents are touched on in the texts, but to a far lesser extent.

Ganesha's rise to prominence was codified in the 9th century when he was formally included as one of the five primary deities of Smartism. The 9th-century philosopher Adi Shankara popularised the "worship of the five forms" (Panchayatana puja) system among orthodox Brahmins of the Smarta tradition. This worship practice invokes the five deities Ganesha, Vishnu, Shiva, Devi, and Surya. Adi Shankara instituted the tradition primarily to unite the principal deities of these five major sects on an equal status. This formalised the role of Ganesha as a complementary deity.

1.18 Scriptures about Lord Ganesha

Once Ganesha was accepted as one of the five principal deities of Hinduism, some Hindus chose Ganesha as their principal deity. They developed the Ganapatya tradition, as seen in the Ganesha Purana and the Mudgala Purana.

The date of composition for the Ganesha Purana and the Mudgala Purana—and their dating relative to one another—has sparked academic debate. Both works were developed over time and contain age-layered strata. It seems likely that the core of the Ganesha Purana appeared around the twelfth and thirteenth centuries, but was later interpolated." The most reasonable date for the Ganesha Purana is considered to be between 1100 and 1400, which coincides with the apparent age of the sacred sites mentioned by the text.

The Mudgala Purana is older than the Ganesha Purana, which dates between 1100 and 1400. While the kernel of the text must be old, it was interpolated until the 17th and 18th centuries as the worship of Ganapati became more important in certain regions. Another highly regarded scripture, the Ganapati Atharvashirsa, was probably composed during the 16th or 17th centuries.

Ganesha Sahasranama is part of the Puranic literature, and is a litany of a thousand names and attributes of Ganesha. Each name in the sahasranama conveys a different meaning and symbolises a different aspect of Ganesha. Versions of the Ganesha Sahasranama are found in the Ganesha Purana.

One of the most important Sanskrit texts that enjoys authority in Ganapatya tradition, is the Ganapati Atharvashirsa.

1.19 Ganesha: Beyond India and Hinduism

Commercial and cultural contacts extended India's influence in Western and Southeast Asia. Ganesha is one of a number of Hindu deities who consequently reached foreign lands.

Ganesha was particularly worshipped by traders and merchants, who went out of India for commercial ventures. From approximately the 10th century onwards, new networks of exchange developed including the formation of trade guilds and a resurgence of money circulation. During this time, Ganesha became the principal deity associated with traders. The earliest inscription invoking Ganesha before any other deity is associated with the merchant community.

Hindus migrated to Maritime Southeast Asia and took their culture, including Ganesha, with them. Statues of Ganesha are found throughout the region, often beside Shiva sanctuaries. The forms of Ganesha found in the Hindu art of Philippines, Java, Bali, and Borneo show specific regional influences. The spread of Hindu culture throughout Southeast Asia established Ganesha worship in modified forms in Burma, Cambodia, and Thailand. In Indochina, Hinduism and Buddhism were practiced side by side, and mutual influences can be seen in the iconography of Ganesha in the region. In Thailand, Cambodia, and among the Hindu classes of the Chams in Vietnam, Ganesha was mainly thought of as a remover of obstacles.

Today in Buddhist Thailand, Ganesha is regarded as a remover of obstacles, the god of success. Thailand regards Ganesha mainly as the god of arts and academics. The belief was initiated by King Vajiravudh of Chakri Dynasty who was devoted to Ganesha personally. He even built a Ganesha shrine at his personal palace, Sanam Chandra

Palace in Nakhon Pathom Province where he focused on his academic and literature works. His personal belief regarding Ganesha as the god of arts formally became prominent following the establishment of the Fine Arts Department where he took Ganesha as the seal. Today, Ganesha is depicted both in the seal of the Fine Arts Department, and Thailand's first prominent fine arts academy; the Silpakorn University.

Before the arrival of Islam, Afghanistan had close cultural ties with India, and the adoration of both Hindu and Buddhist deities was practiced. Examples of sculptures from the 5th to the 7th centuries have survived, suggesting that the worship of Ganesha was then in vogue in the region.

Ganesha appears in Mahayana Buddhism, not only in the form of the Buddhist god Vināyaka, but also as a Hindu demon form with the same name. His image appears in Buddhist sculptures during the late Gupta period. As the Buddhist god Vināyaka, he is often shown dancing. This form, called Nritta Ganapati, was popular in northern India, later adopted in Nepal, and then in Tibet. In Nepal, the Hindu form of Ganesha, known as Heramba, is popular; he has five heads and rides a lion. In one Tibetan form, he is shown being trodden under foot by Mahākāla,(Shiva) a popular Tibetan deity. Other depictions show him as the Destroyer of Obstacles, and sometimes dancing. Ganesha appears in China and Japan in forms that show distinct regional character. In northern China, the earliest known stone statue of Ganesha carries an inscription dated to 531 C.E.. In Japan, where Ganesha is known as Kangiten, the Ganesha cult was first mentioned in 806 C.E.

The canonical literature of Jainism does not mention the worship of Ganesha. However, Ganesha is worshipped by most Jains, for whom he appears to have taken over certain functions of the god of wealth, Kubera. Jain ties with the trading community support the idea that Jainism took up Ganesha worship as a result of commercial connections. The earliest known Jain Ganesha statue dates to about the 9th century. A 15th-century Jain text lists procedures for the installation of its images. Images of Ganesha appear in the Jain temples of Rajasthan and Gujarat.

1.20 108 Names of Lord Ganesha

The Amarakosha, an early Sanskrit lexicon, lists eight synonyms of Ganesha: Vinayaka, Vighnarāja (equivalent to Vighnesha), Dvaimātura (one who has two mothers), Gaṇādhipa (equivalent to Ganapati and Ganesha), Ekadanta (one who has one tusk), Heramba, Lambodara (one who has a pot belly, or, literally, one who has a hanging belly), and Gajanana (gajānana); having the face of an elephant.

Vinayaka (vināyaka) or Binayaka is a common name for Ganesha that appears in the Purāṇas and in Buddhist Tantras. This name is reflected in the naming of the eight famous Ganesha temples in Maharashtra known as the Ashtavinayak (aṣṭavināyaka). The names Vighnesha (vighneśa) and Vighneshvara (vighneśvara) (Lord of Removing Obstacles) refers to his primary function in Hinduism as the master and remover of obstacles (vighna).

A prominent name for Ganesha in the Tamil language is Pillai (Pillaiyar). The two terms are differentiated by saying that pillai means a "child" while pillaiyar means a "noble child". The words pallu, pella, and pell in the Dravidian family of languages signify "tooth or tusk", also "elephant tooth or tusk". The root word pille in the name Pillaiyar might have originally meant "the young of the elephant", because the Pali word pillaka means "a young elephant".

In the Burmese language, Ganesha is known as Maha Peinne, pronounced [məhà pèiʊ̃né]), derived from Pali Mahā Wināyaka. The widespread name of Ganesha in Thailand is Phra Phikanet. The earliest images and mention of Ganesha names as a major deity in present-day Indonesia, Thailand, Cambodia and Vietnam date from the 7th- and 8th-centuries, and these mirror Indian examples of the 5th century or earlier. In Sri Lankan Singhala Buddhist areas, he is known as Gana deviyo, and revered along with Buddha, Vishnu, Skanda and others.

Like other devas (Hindu male deities) and devis (female deities), Ganesha has many other titles of respect or symbolic names.

Here are 108 most popular names of Lord Ganesha:

1. Akhurath: One who has mouse as his charioteer

2. Alampata: Ever eternal lord

3. Amit: Incomparable lord

4. Anantachidrupamayam: Infinite and consciousness personified

5. Avaneesh: Lord of the whole world

6. Avighna: Remover of obstacles

7. Balaganapati: Beloved and lovable child

8. Bhalchandra: Moon-crested lord

9. Bheema: Huge and Gigantic

10. Bhupati: Lord of the gods

11. Bhuvanpati: God of the gods

12. Buddhinath: God of wisdom

13. Buddhipriya: Knowledge bestower

14. Buddhividhata: God of knowledge

15. Chaturbhuj: One who has four arms

16. Devadeva: Lord of all lords

17. Devantakanashakarin: Destroyer of evils and asuras

19. Devendrashika: Protector of all gods

20. Dharmik: One who gives charity

21. Dhoomravarna: Smoke-Hued lord

22. Durja: Invincible lord

23. Dvaimatura: One who has two mothers

24. Ekaakshara: He of the single syllable

25. Ekadanta: Single-Tusked lord

26. Ekadrishta: Single-Tusked lord

27. Eshanputra: Lord Shiva's son

28. Gadadhara: One who has the mace as his weapon

29. Gajakarna: One who has eyes like an elephant

30. Gajanana: Elephant-Faced lord

31. Gajananeti: Elephant-Faced lord

32. Gajavakra: Trunk of the elephant

33. Gajavaktra: One who has mouth like an elephant

34. Ganadhakshya: Lord of all Ganas (Gods)

35. Ganadhyakshina: Leader of all the celestial bodies

36. Ganapati: Lord of all Ganas (Gods)

37. Gaurisuta: The son of Gauri (Parvati)

38. Gunina: One who is the master of all virtues

39. Haridra: One who is golden coloured

40. Heramba: Mother's beloved son

41. Kapila: Yellowish-Brown coloured

42. Kaveesha: Master of poets

43. Kriti: Lord of music

44. Kripalu: Merciful lord

45. Krishapingaksha: Yellowish-Brown eyed

46. Kshamakaram: The place of forgiveness

47. Kshipra: One who is easy to appease

48. Lambakarna: Large-Eared lord

49. Lambodara: The huge bellied lord

50. Mahabala: Enormously strong lord

51. Mahaganapati: Omnipotent and supreme lord

52. Maheshwaram: Lord of the universe

53. Mangalamurti: All auspicious lord

54. Manomay: Winner of hearts

55. Mrityunjaya: Conqueror of death

56. Mundakarama: Abode of happiness

57. Muktidaya: Bestower of eternal bliss

58. Mushikvahana: One who has mouse as charioteer

59. Nadapratithishta: One who appreciates and loves music

60. Namasthetu: Vanquisher of all evils and vices and sins

61. Nandana: Lord Shiva's son

62. Nideeshwaram: Giver of wealth and treasures

63. Omkara: One who has the form of OM

64. Pitambara: One who has yellow-coloured body

65. Pramoda: Lord of all abodes

66. Prathameshwara: First among all

67. Purush: The omnipotent personality

68. Rakta: One who has red-colored body

69. Rudrapriya: Beloved of lord Shiva

70. Sarvadevatman: Acceptor of all celestial offerings

71. Sarvasiddhanta: Bestower of skills and wisdom

72. Sarvatman: Protector of the universe

73. Shambhavi: The son of Parvati

74. Shashivarnam: One who has a moon like complexion

75. Shoorpakarna: Large-eared Lord

76. Shuban: All auspicious lord

77. Shubhagunakanan: One who is the master of all virtues

78. Shweta: One who is as pure as the white colour

79. Siddhidhata: Bestower of success and accomplishments

80. Siddhipriya: Bestower of wishes and boons

81. Siddhivinayaka: Bestower of success

82. Skandapurvaja: Elder brother of Skanda (Lord Kartik)

83. Sumukha: Auspicious face

84. Sureshwaram: Lord of all lords

85. Swaroop: Lover of beauty

86. Tarun: Ageless

87. Uddanda: Nemesis of evils and vices

88. Umaputra: The son of goddess Uma (Parvati)

89. Vakratunda: Curved trunk lord

90. Varaganapati: Bestower of boons

91. Varaprada: Granter of wishes and boons

92. Varadavinayaka: Bestower of success

93. Veeraganapati: Heroic lord

94. Vidyavaridhi: God of wisdom

95. Vighnahara: Remover of obstacles

96. Vignaharta: Demolisher of obstacles

97. Vighnaraja: Lord of all hindrances

98. Vighnarajendra: Lord of all obstacles

99. Vighnavinashanaya: Destroyer of all obstacles and impediments

100. Vigneshwara: Lord of all obstacles

101. Vikat: Huge and gigantic

102. Vinayaka: Lord of all

103. Vishwamukha: Master of the universe

104. Vishwaraja: King of the world

105. Yagnakaya: Acceptor of all sacred and sacrificial offerings

106. Yashaskaram: Bestower of fame and fortune

107. Yashvasin: Beloved and ever popular lord

108. Yogadhipa: The lord of meditation.

1.21 Ganesha as the Formless Divinity

Encapsulated in a magnificent form, for the benefit of the devotee. Gana means group. The universe is a group of atoms and different energies. Just as when atoms bond, matter comes into existence, when all the fragmented aspects of human consciousness bond, Divinity happens effortlessly and that is the birth of Ganesha. This universe would be in chaos if there was no Supreme Law governing these diverse groups of entities. Ganesha is the Lord of all these groups of atoms and energies. He is the Supreme Consciousness that pervades all and brings order in this universe.

While Ganapati is certainly the Nirakara Para Brahman, the formless Reality, He is invoked and worshipped in the form of a mud idol for a period of time for the joy of the devotees. Then Ganapati is asked to merge back into one's heart and the idol is immersed in water. This ritual is observed for the sake of devotees, not for the sake of Ganapati.

The rituals we do outwardly are just to create an atmosphere, to instill a sense of sacredness, especially in children. The real purpose of all this is to bring the vision inwards to the Self. Puja means an act that is born out of fullness ('Pu' for purnata and 'ja' for janma). When you find your inner self, you feel a deep connection with everybody and everything. That fullness and sensitivity begin to come to your experience. Life itself becomes a pooja.

The essence of Ganesha is brought out beautifully by Adi Shankara. Though Ganesha is worshipped as the elephant-headed God, the form is just to bring out its parabrahma roopa. Ganesha is described as Ajam Nirvikalpam Niraakaaramekam. This means that Ganesha is never born. He is Ajam (unborn), he is Niraakaar (formless) and he is Nirvikalpa (attributeless). Ganesha symbolizes the consciousness which is omnipresent.

Ganesha is the same energy which is the reason for this universe, from which everything is manifested and it's the same energy in which the whole world will dissolve. Ganesha is not somewhere outside of us, but the very centre of our life. But this is very subtle knowledge. Not everybody can perceive the formless without the form. Our ancient Rishis and Munis knew this; so they created the form for the benefit and understanding of people at all levels. Those who can't experience the formless, over a period of sustained experience of manifested form reach the formless Brahman.

So in reality, Ganesha is formless; yet there is a form to which Adi Shankara prayed and that form carries the message of the formlessness of Ganesha. Thus, the form serves as the starting point and gradually the formless consciousness begins to manifest. Ganesh Chaturthi marks a unique art of reaching the formless Paramatma called Lord Ganesh by the repeated worship of His manifest form.

Even the Ganesh Stotram, the prayers recited in the praise of Ganeshji, conveys the same. We pray to Ganesha in our consciousness to come out and sit in the idol for us for a while so that we can play with him. After the puja, we again pray asking him to go back to where He came from - our consciousness. While he is in the idol, we offer back whatever God has given us through the puja of the idol.

1.22 Spiritual Consciousness of Ganesha

Spiritual consciousness is omnipresent, yet we are oblivious to it. It's all around us, but few find it. Why? Because the monkey-mind needs to focus on our physical plane through which we can reach spiritual consciousness, especially in troubled times (vighna). This is where the lovable trouble-shooter Ganesha (vighnaharta) steps in. Ancient Indian literature, spiritually and historically refers to Lord Ganesha, the deity of auspicious beginnings. The Ganesha-Purana is named after him while the Skanda-Purana delineates his origin. The Nagdala-Purana says that rishis and munis bowed before this loveable elephant God saying 'Om Ganeshaya Namaha'.

The Yajnavalkya-Smriti describes the cult of the Vinayakas (elephant spirits) who were very mischievous and loved to cause confusion, misery, chaos and untold hindrances. In Hindu temple architecture, the elephant represents the separation of this world from the spiritual-realms. In tantrik symbolism, Ganesha is drawn as a fiery-red triangle (the trinity of the father, son and holy-spirit) set inside a yellow square. In Yoga system, the very first (base) chakra of the human body, called the 'muladhara' is governed by Lord Ganesha. This chakra is the fulcrum of terrific energies which need to be uplifted from the base (sexual) to the sublime. Persons who control and direct this energy (called kundalini) go beyond the ephemeral pleasures of the flesh (called prithvitva to attain soul-knowledge (atma-gyan). Once this base chakra is controlled and then transcended from there to higher chakras, the person evolves very fast spirituality. But as we say in Tao, the journey of a thousand miles begins with the first step. Hence, once this most difficult chakra is transcended, the other six are comparatively easy to deal with and the serpentine-psychic-energy called kundalini can be tapped into quite easily if one is a true seeker.

Ganesha bestows spiritual wisdom since he is the official deity of knowledge. He is also invoked to help mental faculties since he presides over the training of the mind. Perhaps this is why a child's formal education in most Hindu homes always begins with the writing of the words Shri Ganeshya Namaha on the first day of school. Ganesha is called Vinayaka but there is also a female Ganesha called 'Vinayaki'.

The earliest evidence of a female Ganesha or Vinayaki is a weathered terracotta plaque from Rairh in

Rajasthan, which is said to date back to the first century. It is a figure of a corpulent human female body with the elephant head. References to Vinayakis are also abound in the puranas. The Matsya Purana mentions Vinayaki as one of the two hundred 'celestial mothers' created by Mahadev, or Shiva to consume the blood of the fiery demon Andhaka. Linga Purana also mentions the deity. Malini, a demoness, who has an elephant head, drinks Parvati's bath water and is honored by Shiva. Malini, with her elephant head and a human female's body is often said to be the first Vinayaki and is also seen depicted amidst the sculpture of Causath-Yogini temple in Jabalpur, Madhya Pradesh. She stands regally while Ganapati is shown supporting her right foot. Sri Kumara, a text dating back to the sixth century invokes Vinayaki as follows:

Prostrations to the Goddess Vinayaki, who is an elephant above the neck and below is a youthful female. Salutations to Shakti-Ganapati who is vermilion, the colour of the horizon when the sun is about to set, her corpulent belly hangs out enticingly, her breasts bend her waist with their weight and she supports ten splendid arms holding weapons.

The elephant-head can be traced as far back as the genesis of Hinduism when Brahma created the universe from a golden egg called Hiranyagarbha and assigned the duty of guarding the four directions (Dwarpaal) to four elephants. Thus the spiritual consciousness of Ganesha lives even today as a beginner of auspicious new things, a trouble-shooter, bestower of worldly as well as spiritual desires and a guardian who keeps all evil away and lets prosperity enter.

SECTION 2:
LORD GANESHA IN HINDU PURANAS

LORD GANESHA IN 'GANESHA PURANA'

2.1 Lord Ganesha in 'Ganesha Purana'

The 'Ganesha Purana' text presents the mythology and attributes of Hindu deity Ganesha. The Ganesha Purana (gaṇeśa purāṇam) is a Sanskrit text that deals with the Hindu deity Ganesha (Gaṇeśa). It is an upapurāṇa (minor Purana) that includes mythology, cosmogony, genealogy, metaphors, yoga, theology and philosophy relating to Ganesha.

The text is organized in two voluminous sections, one on mythology and genealogy (Krida-khanda, 155 chapters), and the other on theology and devotion (Upasana-khanda, 92 chapters). It exists in many versions. The text's composition and expansion date has been estimated to be the late medieval period, between the 13th- to 18th-century CE, during a period of political turmoil during the Islamic rule period of South Asia. The text shares the features and stories found in all major Puranas, and like all Puranas, it is also a cultural object and reflects the cultural needs and mores, in the environment it was written.

The Ganesha Purana, along with the Mudgala Purana, Brahma Purana and Brahmanda Purana, is one of four Puranic genre encyclopaedic texts that deal with Ganesha. The four texts, two Upa-Puranas and two Maha-Puranas, differ in their focus. The Brahmanda Purana presents Ganesha as Saguna (with attributes and physical form), the Brahma Purana presents Ganesha as Nirguna (without attributes, abstract principle), Ganesha Purana presents him as a union of Saguna and Nirguna concept wherein saguna Ganesha is a prelude to nirguna Ganesha, and the Mudgala Purana describes Ganesha as Samyoga (abstract synthesis with absolute reality and soul).

The Ganesha Purana is an important text particularly for Ganapatyas, who consider Ganesha as their primary deity.

2.2 Significance of Ganesha Purana

The Ganesha Purana is significant because it is, with Ganapati Upanishad, the two most important texts of the Ganapatya sect of Hinduism. The Ganapatyas consider Ganesha as their primary deity, and the mythology of Ganesha found in this Purana is part of their tradition. The text is also significant because it relates to Ganesha, who is the most worshipped god in Hinduism, and revered as the god of beginnings by all major Hindu traditions, namely Shaivism, Vaishnavism, Shaktism and Smartism. The text integrates ancient mythology and Vedantic premises into a Ganesha bhakti (devotional) framework.

The text is also significant to the history of Buddhism and Jainism, since Ganesha is found in their mythologies and theology as well.

2.3 Date of work of Ganesha Purana

The Ganesha Purana and the Mudgala Purana are the two late Puranas (c. AD 1300–1600). The more likely period of composition may be 15th- to 18th-century, during a period of conflict between the Hindu Maratha and Islamic Sultanates in Maharashtra.

The date of composition for both the Ganesha Purana and the Mudgala Purana, and their dating relative to one another, has been a matter of academic debate. Both works contain age-layered strata, but these strata have not been clearly defined through the process of critical editorship. Some strata of the available redactions of the Ganesha Purana and the Mudgala Purana probably reflect mutual influence upon one another, including direct references to one another.

Different views on dating and states her own judgement that it appears likely that the core of the Ganesha Purana came into existence around the 12th and 13th centuries, being subject to interpolations during the succeeding ages. These Puranas, like other Puranas, developed over a period of time as multi-layered works.

The period AD 1100–1400 is the most reasonable date for the Ganesha Purana because that period agrees with the apparent age of the sacred sites in Nagpur and Varanasi areas mentioned by it.

2.4 Structure of Ganesha Purana

The Ganesa Purana is divided into two sections. The Upasanakhanda (upāsanākhaṇḍa) or "section on devotion" has 92 chapters, and the Kridakhanda (krīḍākhaṇḍa) or "section on the divine play (of Gaṇeśa)" has 155 chapters. The Kridakhanda is also called the Uttarakhanda (uttarakhaṇḍa) in the colophons. Chapter 46 of the Upasanakhanda includes a stotra (hymn) that is the source text for one of the best-known versions of the Ganesha Sahasranama (hymn of praise listing 1,000 names and attributes of Ganesha).

The text has five literary units, found in all Puranas: khanda, mahatmya, upakhyana, **gita** and a narrative unit. It is structured as a recitation by sage Vyasa, traceable to sages in the mythical Naimisa forest in Hinduism. The composition style is didactic (in the manner of a teacher) and mythic, the imagery and framing of story is similar to the other Puranas. The text has four idiosyncrasies, in that it contains no pancalaksana content, minimal didactic presentation of dharmashastra, the myths are structured as involving Ganesha's intervention in ancient Hindu mythology, and the mythical plots invariably present Ganesha as the life and inner principle of all other Hindu deities.

2.5 Contents of Ganesha Purana

The Upasanakhanda, or the first part of the Ganesha Purana, presents two modes of worship. One is meditation and mystic contemplation of Ganesha as the eternal Brahman presented in Vedanta school of Hindu philosophy, the metaphysical absolute and Paramatma (Nirguna, supreme spirit), where he is same as the Atman (soul, innermost self) within oneself. The second approach, suggests the Ganesapurana, is through preparing an image of god (Saguna, murti), decorating it with flowers, presenting it offerings and festively remembering him in Puja-style homage. The Upasanakhanda presents these ideas in a series of episodical stories and cosmogony, that weaves in ancient mythologies as dynamic empirical reality and presents Ganesha as the Vedantist Brahman, or the absolute unchanging reality.

2.6 Kridakhanda: The Ganesha Gita

Chapters 138-48 of the Kridakhanda constitute the Ganesha Gita, which is modelled on the Bhagavad Gita, but adapted to place Ganesha in the divine role. The discourse is given to King Varenya during Ganesha's incarnation as Gajanana.

2.6.1 Know your soul

Ganesha said, "The man who delights in his own self and is attached to his own self, attains bliss and indestructible happiness, for there is no happiness in the senses. Enjoyments which arise from the objects of the senses are the causes of pain and are connected to birth and destruction. The wise man is not attached to them. (...)

Grounded within the soul, shining within the soul, happy with the soul, he who delights in the soul, will certainly gain the imperishable Brahman and bring about the good aims of all people. (...)

Mark! For all those who know their own self, Brahman shines everywhere. (...)

—Ganesha Purana, Krida Khanda, 142.21 - 142.26

The Ganesha Gita shows that ninety percent of its stanzas are, with slight modifications, taken from the Bhagavad Gita. Their topics are the same: karma yoga, jnana yoga and bhakti yoga. However, Ganesha replaces Krishna in the divine role, states Yuvraj Krishan.

While Bhagavad Gita is a strong possible source, the Ganesha Gita, it has only 412 verses in this section and skips a large number of verses in Bhagavad Gita, and it is incorrect to presume that the text is identical in all respects and merely replaces Ganesha for Krishna. The discussion develops differently, and the character of Varenya is far weaker than the inquisitive philosophical questions of Arjuna in the Bhagavad Gita, as Varenya asks questions of Ganesha. However the theology found in Bhagavad Gita and Ganesha Gita are substantially the same.

2.7 Kridakhanda: Ganesha in four Yugas (Four Avatars of Ganesha)

The Kridakhanda of the Ganesha Purana narrates the stories of four incarnations (Avatars) of Ganesha, each for the four different yugas. The 155 chapters of this section are separated into the four yugas. Chapters 1 through 72 present Ganesha in Satya Yuga, chapters 73 through 126 present Ganesha's story in the Treta Yuga, while chapters 127 through 137 present his stories in Dvapara Yuga. **Chapter 138 through 148 present the Ganesha Gita**, followed by a short section on Kali Yuga (current age) in chapter 149. The rest of chapter 149 through chapter 155 are interlocutory, following the literary requirements of a valid Puranic genre.

According to the Ganesha Purâna, four Ganesh incarnations (avatars) came on earth during the different yuga's, in order to fight the demons. They are :

(i) **Mahotkata** with ten arms, seated on a lion, shining like the sun, came during the Krita Yuga to kill the demons Narântak and Devântak

(ii) White-coloured **Shri Mayureshvar** with six arms, riding the peacock, faced the demon Sindhu during the Treta Yuga

(iii) Red-colored **Shri Gajânana** with four arms, mounted on his rat, destroyed the demon Sindur during the Dwapara Yuga

(iv) Dhûmraketu is the form of Ganesh who will come in the future; we are now living in the Kali Yuga. Two-arms and smoke-coloured Dhûmraketu will ride on a blue horse; he will fight all the devils to restore peace and harmony in the world.

2.8 Thirty-Two Manifestations (Forms) of Ganapati (Vinayagar)

According to Ganesha Purana, Vinayagar is described in 32 different forms or manifestations; however, Maha Ganapati is the most commonly worshipped form. In the light of the Vinayagar Chaturthi celebrations, let us take a look at the 32 forms of Vinayagar.

1. Bala Ganapati

As the name suggests, Bala Ganapati is the child form of Vinayagar that symbolizes earth's abundance and fertility as he holds a banana, mango, sugarcane, and jackfruit in each of His four hands. His trunk curls around His favourite sweet 'Modakam'.

Karastha kadali chootha, panasekshuka modhakam,
Bala soorya prabhakaram, vandeham bala ganapathim,

Meaning: I salute the boy like Ganapathi who shines like a young Sun, Holding in his hands Banana fruit, mango fruit, jack fruit, sugarcane and Modhaka.

2. Taruna Ganapati

Taruna Ganapati is in His teens and symbolizes youthfulness (His body glows in red). In this form, Vinayagar has 8 arms, each holding a modakam, noose, goad, wood apple, rose apple, tusk, some paddy, and sugar cane.

Pasangusa apoopa kapitha jamboo phalam thilan venumapiswa hasthai,

Drutha sadasya tharuna arunabha paayath sayushmaan tharuno Ganesha.

Meaning: Long live the Teen aged Ganapathi who holds the noose, goad, jaggery sweet,

Wood apple, rose apple, Gingili and cane, Who wears the shining red colour of dawn and gets you very long life.

3. Bhakti Ganapati

As Bhakti Ganapati, Vinayagar holds a banana, a mango, coconut and a bowl of sweet payasam pudding in each of His four arms. The divine sight of this form shines like a full moon and usually worshipped by farmers during harvest season.

Nalikeramra kadali gula payasa dharinam,
Sarthchandra bhava pusham, bhaje bhaktha ganapathim.

Meaning: I salute the devotee Ganapathi, who shines like the autumn moon, Holding in his hands coconut, mango, banana and a pot of Jaggery Payasam.

4. Vira Ganapati

Vira Ganapati is a 16-armed warrior holding weapons in His arms—signifying Vinayagar's triumph over evil and ignorance.

Vethala sakthi sara karmuka chakra gadvanga, mudgara, gadhaam angusa naga pasaan,

Soolam cha kuntha parasu dwajam udvahantham, veeram Ganeshamarunam sathatham smaraami.

Meaning: I always, meditate on the red valorous Ganapathi who holds goblin, spear, bow, arrow, hammer, mace, Wheel, sword, shield, mace, goad, snake, noose, trident, pick axe, battle axe and flag.

5. Shakti Ganapati

In this form, Vinayagar is a protector as one of His 'shaktis' is seated on His lap. On the other hand, Shakti Ganapati holds an 'Abhaya mudra', bestowing blessings to all His devotees.

Aalinghya devim harithaam nishannam parasparaslishta katou nivesaya,
Sandhyarunaam pasa sruneem vahantham bhayapaham Shakthi Ganapathi meede.

Meaning: I salute the Ganapathi with Shakthi, who is seen embracing his wife, Who holds a green lemon, who and his wife seated on his knee embrace each other, Who is of the orange colour of the dusk, who holds the tusk and goad and shows sign of protection.

6. Dvija Ganapati

This four-headed Dvija Ganapati is worshipped for wealth and knowledge. 'Dvija' means twice born. In this form, Vinayagar holds a 'Kamandalu', Rudraksha, a staff, and a leaf scripture.

Ya pusthakaksha guna dhanda kamandalu sreenirvruthyamana kara bhooshana mindu varnam,

Sthambera manana chathushtaya shobhamanam thwaam samsmare dwija ganathipathe dhanya

Meaning: I remember the honorable twice-born Ganesha, who holds book of palm leaves, a staff, water pot, Who is happy and decorates his hands by a moon, and who shines like the four-legged elephant.

7. Pingala (Siddhi) Ganapati

Glowing in golden yellow, Siddhi Ganapati is the master of intellect and success. Sitting in a relaxed position, this form of Vinayagar holds a bouquet of flowers, an axe, mango, sugar cane and, in His trunk, a modakam.

Pakva chootha kalpa manjarim ikshu danda thila modhakai saha,

Udwahan parasu hastha they Nama sri samrudhipatha deva Pingala.

Meaning: Salutations to the reddish brown coloured god armed with axe in his hand, who signifies plenty, Who holds ripe mango, bouquet of turmeric, sugarcane and sesame sweet.

8. Ucchhishta Ganapati

Ucchhishta Ganapati is called the 'Lord of Blessed Offerings' and is the guardian of culture. 'Shakti' of creativity sits on His laps and His hands carry the veena, a blue lotus, pomegranate, meditation beads and a stalk of paddy.

Neelabjam dadimi veena saali gunjaksha suthrakam,

Dadadad uchishta naamaayam Ganesha pathu mokshadha

Meaning: Let The Ganapathi called the Ganapathi who gives the left over; Who holds a blue lotus, Pomegranate, Veena, rosary

9. Vighna Ganapati

Vighna Ganapati means remover of obstacles. Just like Lord Vishnu, this eight-armed form of Vinayagar has a Shankhu and Chakra in two of His hands. In others, He holds a noose, goad, tusk, modakam, a bouquet of flowers, sugar cane, flower arrow, and an axe.

Pasangusa swadam thamra phalavaan aaghu vahana,

Vighnan nihanthu rakthavarno vinayaka.

Meaning: Let the blood red coloured Ganesha who holds the rope and goad; Own tusk and mango and rides on a mouse remove my obstacles.

10. Kshipra Ganapati

It's believed that Kshipra Ganapati is the giver of boons. In this form, Vinayagar is known to fulfill His devotees' wishes quickly. He carries a noose, goad and a sprig of the kalpavriksha (wish-fulfilling tree). A pot of jewels is seen curled up in His trunk.

Danthakalpa lathaapasa rathna kumbham kusojjwalam,

Bandhooka kamaneeyamam dhyayeth kshipra ganadhipam.

Meaning: I meditate on the easily pleased Lord of Ganas who holds a blue lotus and shining sprig of paddy; Who holds a climbing plant, rope, gem studded pot and as pretty as Bandhooka tree.

11. Heramba Ganapati

Vinayagar is a five-faced protector who rides a lion in this form called Heramba Ganapati. He carries an axe, hammer, noose, beads, broken tusk, garland, fruit and modakam in eight of His ten hands.

Abhaya varada hastha pasaa danthakshamala sruni parasudhano mudgaram modhakam cha,

Phalam adhigatha Simha Pancha mathanga vakthro Ganapathi rathi gaura, pathu heramba nama.

Meaning: Let me be protected by the five-elephant headed Ganesha riding on a lion who is very serious, who is called Heramba, Who shows signs of protection and boons, who holds the rope, his tusk, rosary, sickle, axe, hammer, citron, and Modhaka.

12. Lakshmi Ganapati

His shaktis Buddhi and Siddhi seated on Vinayagar's laps in this form is actually wisdom and achievement. Two of His hands gesture the Varadha and Abhaya Mudras, while other hands bear a green Parrot, a Pomegranate, a sword, a noose, elephant goad, sprig of Kalpavriksha (Wish-fulfilling tree) and water vessel. Both His shaktis hold white lotus flowers.

Vibrana suka bhjeeja poora kamalam,
manikhya kumbha angusan,

Pasam kalpa lathaancha gadga vilasath
jjyothi sudhaa nirjjara,

Shyamenatha saroruhena sahitho devi dvayenaanthike,

Gourangavara dhannaa hastha kamalo
Lakshmi ganeso avathath.

Meaning: All over is spread the white Lakshmi Ganesha who holds a parrot, pomegranate, lotus flower, Gem studded pot, goad, noose, the wish giving creeper, sword and shines like a flame fulfilling all wishes. Sits near a blue lotus filled lake along with his two consorts and shows the boon giving hand.

13. Maha Ganapati

The most commonly-worshipped form of Vinayagar. It's believed that the worshippers of Maha Ganapati will gain intellect, prosperity and protection from evil. Seated together with one of His shaktis, Maha Ganapati holds His broken tusk, blue lily, lotus, a pomegranate, a stalk of sugarcane, sprig of paddy and weapons.

Hastheendranana indhu chooda aruna chayaam trinethram rasath,

Aaslishtam priyayaa sapadma karaya swangasthaaya santhatham,

Bheejapoora gadhekshu karmukalasachakrabhja pasothphala,

Breehyagraswa vishana rathna kalasaan hasthair vahantham bhaje.

Meaning: I sing about The great Ganapathi who is of red colour, who has a face of king of elephants, Who wears the moon, has three eyes, , embraces always his darling sitting on his lap with his lotus like hands, Who holds pomegranate, mace, sugarcane, a pot of jewels, discuss, blue lotus flower, rope, broken tusk and pot of jewels.

14. Vijaya Ganapati

Vijayam means victory. Sitting on top of Mooshika (His vehicle mouse), Vijaya Ganapati is the destroyer of dark forces. His four arms carry a broken tusk, noose, goad, and a ripe mango.

Pasangusa swadam thamra phalavaan aaghu vahana,

Vighnan nihanthu rakthavarno vinayaka.

Meaning: Let the blood red coloured Ganesha who holds the rope and goad, Own tusk and mango and rides on a mouse remove my obstacles.

15. Nritya Ganapati

With a golden glow, Nritya Ganapati is the Dancer—joyfully vibrant! Dancing under the kalpavriksha (wish-fulfilling tree); he wears rings on His fingers while the four arms bear the tusk, noose, goad, and modakam.

Pasangusa poopoa kutara dandha, chanchatkara kluptha varanguleeyakam,

Peetha prabham kalpa tharor adhastham bhajami nruthopapadham Ganesham.

Meaning: I sing about the dancing Ganesha, who is of yellow golden color, who sits below wish giving tree, Who holds the noose, goad, Modhaka, tusk, shining divine rings arranged on his fingers.

16. Urdhva Ganapati

Urdhava Ganapati is the 'elevated one' who's sitting in a tantric position with His shakti. Each of His six hands bears a lotus, paddy, sugarcane, an arrow, broken tusk, and blue lily.

Kalhari shali kamalekshuka chapa bana Dantha prorahaka gadhi kanakojjawalanga,

Aalinganodhyatha karo harithanga yashtya devya disathw abhayam oordhwa ganathipo may.

Meaning: Let me be given protection by the upright Ganapathi, who embraces his Shakthi who sits on his left thigh. Who is of golden colour, who holds a blue lily, lotus flower, sugarcane, bow and arrows, a sprig of paddy and the club.

17. Ekakshara Ganapati

Sitting on His divine vehicle Mooshika in the Padmashana pose, Ekakshara Ganapati is a four-armed and three-eyed form of Vinayagar. He holds a noose, goad and a pomegranate in His hands.

Raktho rakthangaragaam Shuka, kusumayutha thundhila chandra mouli,

Nethrair yuktha sthribhi Vamana kara charano bheeja pooram dadhaana,

Hasthaagra kluptha pasangusa sharada varadho naga vakthrohi bhoosho,

Deva padmasanastho bhavathu Sukha karo bhoothaye vighna raja.

Meaning: Let us be granted pleasant life by the king of obstacles, who is red and wears red cloths, Who holds a parrot and lotus and wears the crescent on his crown, Who has three eyes, who holds pomegranate on his left hand, Who holds the rope and the goad in his hands, decorates himself with a snake and grants clear boons.

18. Varada Ganapati

Varada Ganapati fulfills His devotees' wishes. Just like His father Lord Shiva, Varada Ganapati has the third eye of wisdom and a crescent moon over His head. He also bears a noose, goad, dish of honey in His hands and a pot of jewels in His trunk.

Sindhoorabhamibhanam trinayanam, cha pasamguso,

Bhibranaam Madhu math kapalam anisam sadvindu moulim bhaje,

Prushtayaa aslishta thanum dwajagra karayaa padmollasaddhasthayaa,

Thadhonyahitha pani mathava vasumath pathrolasad pushkaram.

Meaning: I pray Lord Ganesha who is of lustrous colour of saffron, who has three eyes. Who has noose and goad, Who always carries honey in a skull and has crescent on his crown and Who sits embracing his wife carrying lotus and a flag, With his fourth hand caressing her thighs, And his trunk carrying a pot of jewels.

19. Tryakshara Ganapati

Tryakshara Ganapati is the Lord of A-U-M. He carries the broken tusk, goad, noose and mango in His hands and a modakam in His trunk.

Gajendra vadanam sakshad chala karna suchamaram,

Hema varnam chathur bahumn pasangusa daram varam,

Swadantham dakshine hasthe savye thwamraphalam thadhaa,

Pushkare modhakam chaiva darayanthamanusmareth.

Meaning: I remember that Ganapathi with elephant face, whose ears are like fans, Who is golden in colour, who has four hands, who carried a rope and a goad, Who carries his own tusk in right hand and also a mango fruit, And also carries a Modhaka by his tusk.

20. Kshipra Prasada Ganapati

This form of Vinayagar rests on a Kusha grass throne. He fulfills His devotees' wishes quickly but punishes any wrongdoings even quicker. While His big belly symbolizes the universe, while His arms bear a broken tusk, the twig of Kalpavriksha, noose, an elephant goad, pomegranate, and a white lotus.

Drutha pasangusa kalpa latha swaradhascha bheejapoorayuthaa,

Sasi sakala kalitha mouli strilochano arunascha, gaja vadana,

BHasura bhoosgana deeptho brahad dara padmam vishtarollasitha,

Vighna payodhara pavana kara drutha kamla sadhasthu bruthyai.

Meaning: I pray for prosperity that Ganesha who holds the rope, goad, wish giving creeper, his own tusk and pomegranate, Who has crescent decorating his crown, who has three eyes, who is red in colour and has an elephant face, Who has a big form decorated by ornaments and is happy with the big lotus flower he holds, Who removes all obstacles by his grace like wind using the lotus flower that he holds.

21. Haridra Ganapati

Seated on a royal throne, this calm-faced Haridra Ganapati clad in golden yellow vest and ornaments holds a broken tusk, modakam, noose and a goad in His hands.

Haridram chathur bahum, haridra vadanam prabhum,

Pasangusa daram devam modakam danthameva cha,

Bhakthabhaya pradatharam vandhe vigna vinasanam.

Meaning: I salute the dispeller of obstacles, who protects his devotees, Who is yellow in colour, has four hands, who is the lord having golden face, Who is the god holds noose, goad, Modhaka and the tusk.

22. Ekadanta Ganapati

Compared to the other forms, Ekadanta Ganapati has a bigger belly and is known for His broken tusk. His hands hold broken tusk, Laddu, japa beads mala, and an axe to cut the bond of ignorance.

Lambhodaram, shyama thanum Ganesham
kutaramakshasraja moordwagabhyam,

Saladrungum danthamadha karabhyaam
vametharabhyam cha dadhana meede.

Meaning: I salute Ganesha, who has a big paunch, who has a black body who holds an axe and a rosary, Who is upright and has his broken trunk in his left hands.

23. Srishti Ganapati

Srishti Ganapati is the happy form of Vinayagar. He holds a noose, a goad, a perfect mango, and His tusk, representing selfless sacrifice.

Pasangusa swadantha aamra phalavan aaghu vahana,

Vighnan nihanthu nassona srushti daksho vinayaka.

Meaning: Let the blood red coloured Ganesha who holds the rope and goad, Own tusk and mango and rides on a mouse and, Who is engaged in creation of beings with blood, remove my obstacles.

24. Uddanda Ganapati

Uddanda Ganapati enforces justice. Accompanied by one of His shaktis, this is an angry form of Vinayagar. In His ten hands, he carries a pot of jewels, a blue lily, sugar cane, mace, lotus flower, a sprig of paddy, pomegranate, noose, garland, and His broken tusk.

Kalhurambuja bheeja pooraka gadha danthekshu banaissadaa,

Bhibrano mani khumba Sali kalaso paasam cha chakranvitham,

Gowarangyaa ruchiraa aravindha karayaa devyaa sadaa samyuthaa,

Sonangusa shubha mathanothu bajathaam udhanda vigneswaraa.

Meaning: I sing about the extraordinary (unchained) Ganesha with a prayer for all that is good, who is red in colour; Who holds blue lily, Pomegranate, mace, broken tusk, sugarcane, arrow, pot of gems, rope, lotus paddy ear, goad and the wheel, And who is always with his wife holding a white-coloured lotus and sitting on his lap.

25. Rinamochana Ganapati

Rinamochana Ganapati frees His devotees from guilt and bondage by giving 'moksha'. He wields a noose, goad, rose apple and broken tusk in His four hands.

Pasangusou dantha jambu dadhana spatika prabha,

Rakthamsuko Ganapathir mudhesyadh runa mochaka.

Meaning: Let the Ganapathi of crystal colour dressed in red holding rope, goad and rose apple. Happily remove all my bondage and loans.

26. Dhundhi Ganapati

Dhundh means search. This is the form of Vinayar sought after by the devotees. He is the symbol of awakening. Dhundhi Ganapati holds a strand of rudraksha beads, His broken tusk, an axe, and a small pot of jewels.

Akshmaalaam kutaaram cha rathna pathram swadanthakam,

Dathe karair vighna rajo dundi nama mudhesthuna.

Meaning: Does not the dispeller of obstacles, who is called Dundi, Holding a rosary, sword, pot of gems and his own tusk is joyfully sought after.

27. Dvimukha Ganapati

In this form, Vinayagar has two faces enabling Him to see in all directions. Dvimukha Ganapati's four arms hold the goad, noose, a pot of gems and His broken tusk symbolising self-sacrifice.

Swadantha pasangusa rathna pathram, karair dadhano Harineelagra gathra,

Rakthamsuko rathna kireeta mali bhoothyai sadaa may dwimukho Ganesha.

Meaning: I salute always for my sake the Ganesha who has two faces, Who is bluish green and wears red cloth and wearing a garland a red crown, And holds in his hand, His own tusk, rope goad, pot of gems.

28. Trimukha Ganapati

Just like His name, this form of Vinayagar is three-faced and bestows protection and blessings to His devotees. Resting on a golden lotus, this six-armed Trimukha Ganapati bears a noose, goad, beads and a pot of nectar.

Srimath theeshna siravangusa aksha varadhan dakshedadhana karai.

Panchamrutha poorna kumbham abhayam vaame dadhanomudhaa,

Peeta swarnamayaravindha vilasath sathkarnikaa bhasure,

AAseena strimukha palaasa ruchiro nagaanaana pathunaa.

Meaning: Let me be protected by three faced Ganesha with elephant face shining like the flame of the forest, Who holds on his right hand, a very sharp shining hook, a rosary and the signing of blessing, Who holds in a right hand a full pot of nectar and sign of protection, And who sits on a golden throne with lotus inlaid wearing a shining ear ring.

29. Simha Ganapati

Sinha Ganapati is fearless as he rides and holds lions to signify strength and boldness. He also carries a kalpavriksha (wish-fulfilling tree) sprig, the vina, a lotus blossom, flower bouquet and a pot of jewels.

Veenaam kalpa lathaam arincha varadam
dakshe vidathe karai,

Vame thamarasamcha rathna kalasam sanmanjari
chabhayam,

Shunda danda lasath mrugendra vadana
sankhendu giwara shubha,

Dheevyath rathna nibhamsuko Ganapathi
payadapayath sanaha.

Meaning: Let me protected from all dangers, by the Ganapathi who shines like gems, Who holds on his right hand veena, wish giving creeper and protection to even enemies, Who holds on his left hand a pot of gems, a bouquet of flowers and sign of protection, Who shines like a white conch and a moon and is lion faced along with elephant trunk.

30. Yoga Ganapati

As the name suggests, Vinayagar resembles a yogi in this form. Glowing like the morning sun, Yoga Ganapati is seen meditating while His hands hold a stalk of sugar cane, a staff, prayer beads, and a noose.

Yogaroodo yoga pattabhi ramo balarkabhaschensra neelamsu kadaya,

Paseeswakshaan yoga dandam dadhanopaya nithyam yoga vigneswarona.

Meaning: I daily salute the Yoga Ganesha, who sits on a yogic pose, crowned as master of yoga, Who shines like sun, wears blue cloths and holds rope, rosary and Yoga staff.

31. Durga Ganapati

As Durga Ganapati, Vinayagar symbolizes triumph over darkness. In this form, He bears a bow, arrow, noose, goad, prayer beads, broken tusk and a rose apple in His hands.

Thaptha kanchana sankaaschath ashta hastho mahath thanu,

Deepthangusam sarancha aksham dantham dakshe vahan karai,

Vaame pasam karmukam chalatham jambudayathath karai,

Rakthamsuka sadaa bhooyath Durga ganapathir mudhe.

Meaning: Let me be kept always happy by Durga Ganapathi who wears red cloths, Who is of the colour of molten gold with a huge body having eight hands, Who holds an arrow, shining goad, rosary and his tusk on his right hands, And who holds a noose, a bow, a wish giving creeper and rose apple.

32. Sankatahara Ganapati

Sankatahara Ganapati eliminates all sorts of sorrows and difficulties. As Vinayagar sits on a red lotus in this form, He carries noose, goad and a bowl of payasam in His hands. His right-hand shows Varadha mudra to bestow blessings to the devotees.

Balarkaaruna kanthir vaame Baalaam vaha nankhe,

Lasad indhivara hastham gourangim rathna shobhadyaam,

Dakshe angusa varadhanam vame pasancha Payasam pathram,

Neelaam Shuka samana peedepadhyarune thishtan,

Sankataharana paayath sankatapoogadh gajanano nithyam.

Meaning: Let my sorrows be daily destroyed by Sankata Hara Ganapathi, Who shines red like the infant sun who has on his left lap his wife, Carrying a pretty lotus and shining with radiance and wearing jewels, Who carries on his right hand a goad and sign of blessing, And in his left hand a rope, pot of Payasam and is seated, On a red lotus flower wearing blue cloths.

2.9 Manuscripts Related to Ganesha

There are hundreds of manuscripts for this Purana in libraries in India, and that it was clearly very popular from the 17th to 19th centuries. The Upasanakhanda (upāsanākhaṇḍa) was published in 1979 and the Kridakhanda (krīḍākhaṇḍa) was published in 1985.

2.10 Ganesha Gita from 'Ganesha Purana'

Varenya said, 'In the world of birth and death many difficulties arise, and they are very hard to endure. Remover of obstacles, kindly show me the path to liberation now. How can there be bondage in the realization of You. Declare to me that teaching by which I will attain liberation, that yoga through which I will give up desire, anger and the fear of death.'

Brahma said, "After having listened to this speech, Gajanana kindly sat Varenya on a comfortable seat and placed his hand on his head. Then he began to teach him the Ganesha Gita, casting away all his doubts by presenting His universal form. As soon as he understood the essence of the Gita from Ganesha's instruction and having transferred the kingdom to his ministers, he went to the forest. Filled with detachment, the accomplished King meditated on Gajanana, fixed on nothing else, and always preached the Gita.

Just as water thrown into water stays only as water, so he came to consist of Him by meditating on Him.'

Vyasa said, 'Four-faced one, Lord of the gods, recite the Ganesha Gita with the highest compassion. For it removes all ignorance.'

Brahma said, "This very thing was previously requested by the great Saunaka Rishi. The sage recited the Gita as he had heard it from Vyasa's mouth."

Chapter 1

Saunaka said, 'You have tasted this nectar which is told in the eighteen Puranas. I also wish to drink this supreme nectar that has an extraordinary taste, with which na man, having been filled with this nectar attains the Supreme Brahman. Blessed one, tell me compassionately about that nectar of this yoga.'

Vyasa said, 'Herewith I will tell you that Gita which presents the path of yoga. Saunaka, it was entrusted to that inquisitive king by the elephant-faced God.'

Varenya said, 'Lord of obstacles, mighty-armed God, who is skilled in all the sciences, and who knows the true meaning of all the sacred texts, please tell me about this yoga.'

Gajanana said, 'O King, your intention has been well determined through my favour. I am going to tell you that Gita which consists of the nectar of yoga. They say that this yoga is not the yoga of prosperity, nor obtainable through the objects of the senses, nor obtainable through the material elements either. The union of mother and father is not yoga, overlord of men, nor is the union with sons, kinsmen and others, nor is it the yoga with its eightfold mystic powers. It is not the yoga of union with women as stated in the sutras. Nor is it the yoga of sovereignty over a kingdom, nor the yoga of controlling elephants and horses, nor the union with Indra's world, nor the yoga loved by those whose goal is yoga, nor do I consider that yoga union with the heavenly realms. Yoga is not union with Siva's abode, nor with the abode of Visnu. This yoga does not pertain to Surya, Chandra, nor Kubera, nor Vayu, nor Agni, nor to become immortal, nor to surpass time, nor to become Varuna or Nirriti, nor to reign over the entire earth.

Those without true spiritual knowledge practice yoga, Protector of the earth, which is of various kinds. In the world those who have truly attained yoga have overcome hunger, thirst and the desire for progeny. They purify all the worlds and have brought the three worlds under their control. Their hearts are filled with compassion and they enlighten everyone. They are liberated whilst alive and are immersed in the pool that has the form of the highest bliss. After closing their eyes they see the Supreme Brahman in their heart. They meditate on the Supreme Brahman who has appeared in their heart by this yoga. They consider all beings to be identical

with their own self. With their hearts filled with compassion, they wander on the Earth irrespective of whether anyone cuts or strikes them, whether anyone is attracted to them or whether anyone seeks refuge with them. For the purification of all living beings, their anger and senses conquered, they merely carry their bodies. Protector of the earth, a mound of dirt and gold are the same to them. Those who come into contact with such a rare soul are very fortunate, dearest one.

I will tell you about this excellent yoga. Listen attentively, for hearing about it a man is released from evil acts and from the ocean of material existence. Any yoga involving a fixed mind resting on Siva, Visnu, Shakti, Surya and on me, protector of men, is the right yoga in my opinion. I alone, having taken various forms, create, protect and destroy the world for my own play. I alone am Maha Visnu, I alone am Sadasiva, I alone am the great Shakti, I alone am Aryaman, dear one. I alone am the Lord of men who previously appeared as the five principle incarnations.

Because they are ignorant they do not know me as the cause of the cause of the world. I am considered to be fire, water, earth and I am considered to be ether and air, Brahma, Visnu, Rudra, the world protectors and all the directions, the Vasus, the Maruts, the cows, the sages and the animals, rivers, oceans, yaksas, trees and flocks of birds, and the twenty-one heavens, the snakes and the seven forests, humans, mountains, the sadhyas, perfected beings and hosts of rakshasas. I am the witness, the eye of the world, untouched by all actions, the unchangeable, the immeasurable, I am the un-manifest, omnipresent and imperishable. I alone am the Supreme Brahman who possesses everlasting bliss, King.

My power of maya deludes all these excellent men. The material elements are perceived by the six senses. A person should always concentrate intensely on Me, after gradually leaving behind the veil of illusion over many births. After becoming indifferent to the objects of the senses, one should know Brahman through right knowledge. Brahman cannot be cut by strokes of a sword, nor burnt by fire, nor can it be made wet by living creatures, nor dried up by the wind. Nor can it be killed, even when the body is destroyed, Protector of men. Those ignorant people who are obsessed with the Vedas praise the flowery words uttered in the Vedas and think of nothing other than that. They always engage in activities that produce birth and death as its result. They are obsessed with power and heaven; their minds are scattered and their intellect absorbed in carnal enjoyment. They produce their own bondage by themselves, Protector of the Earth.

Those ignorant men obsessed with activity are joined to the wheel of samsara. One engaged in activity should do it and offer the results to Me, because the huge sprouts of the seeds of karma will be cut off for him. His mind will be greatly purified. and he will gain spiritual knowledge. The Supreme Brahman is known (by the sages) through this knowledge. Therefore, Overlord of men, one should perform actions with the intellect absorbed in Me. But nobody should not act and abandon his own duty. If one gives up actions, then one will not find success. Initially he has no command over knowledge and it is appropriate to focus on action. One whose heart is purified by action achieves a unified intellect. Moreover, that yoga is declared to be conducive to the state of immortality.

I will describe another yoga. Hear about it, Protector of the Earth, as it is superb. A man should see with equal vision in an animal, a son, a friend, an enemy, kinsman and a good friend. With detachment he should have the same attitude towards joy, pain, patience, elation and fear, sickness, carnal enjoyments, victory and defeat, acquisition and loss of wealth. In gain and loss and in death, he is the same and sees Me within and outside all things. Who sees Me always in Surya, Soma, water, fire, Siva, Shakti, in the heavenly musicians, humans and the lower creatures, he is the knower of yoga, it is said. And within the brahmin, in the heart, in the great river, in the sacred ford, in the sacred place, in the removal of evil, in Visnu, in all the gods, and Yakshas and Uragas.

After comprehensively removing the senses from their own objects by means of discrimination, the intellect assumes impartiality in regard to everything. I consider this to be yoga, Protector of the Earth. Through the discrimination of the self by the self the intellect of that man, attached to his own duty, emerges by the power of providence. Hence it is that yoga that is said to be real yoga. United with the intellect, a man now abandons both action and non-action. After that, he should continually practice yoga. Yoga is prosperity in what is enjoined in the sastras. After giving up the results both action and non-action, a man of integrity, his senses conquered, is freed from bondage and birth and goes to the salubrious place. When a man's intellect will overcome the turbidity of ignorance, then he gradually becomes dispassionate towards the words of the Vedas and so forth. When the intellect of that person whose mind diverges from the three Vedas becomes stable and rests on the Supreme Self, then he attains yoga. When a wise man gives up all the desires in his mind, dear king, wholly satisfied with himself in his own self, then his intellect is said to be firm.

The man who has no desire in respect of any of his friends and who is not agitated when encountering pain, and who is without fear, pain or passion, is then said to have a firm intellect. Just as the tortoise contracts its limbs, so too should a person, absorbed in yoga withdraws his own senses from their objects. The objects of the senses disperse for the embodied person who fasts. He comes to be without passion and when passion disappears he will see Brahman. On assuming the steadiness of the yogi, the learned person always strives for yoga (because the senses which become agitated can at any time forcibly draw away the mind). The man who is self-controlled and has brought the senses under control will always be absorbed in Me.

Whoever have their senses restrained are considered to be one who have attained intelligence. For the person who reflects on the objects of the senses, attachment to them arises. Desire then arises and anger increases from that. From anger ignorance arises, then loss of memory. From loss of memory, there is a failure in correct thinking. From that, his spiritual life is ruined. Without hatred, passion and the objects of the senses, that man should act through the senses. The heart, which is free from the control of the senses, increases its satisfaction. When one is satisfied there will be a casting away of the three kinds of pain. And the person who has situated himself within wisdom will have a peaceful heart. Without peace, there is no correct thinking. And without that, there is no contemplation, there is no peace, and without peace where does happiness come from? Since the mind follows the senses, which are like horses wandering after their objects, it will, therefore, destroy correct thinking, like the wind destroys a boat in water. What is night for all beings, he never slumbers. What is day for all beings, that is his night, Protector of the earth. Just as rivers come to the ocean from everywhere, so one who has material desires will never have peace. Therefore, after the man has completely blocked the senses from everything in the world, they flee from their objects and his intellect is then firm. After giving up all thoughts of 'Me-ness' and 'I-ness', he should give up all his desires and should then focus on intuitive knowledge. From intuitive knowledge he will become liberated.

Protector of the Earth, you are he who knows the wisdom of Brahman because of fate, and after obtaining yoga you will become liberated by your nature." Om. This is the truth. This is called 'The Essence of Sankhya Yoga' in the conversation between Lord Ganesha and King Varenya in the Uttarakhanda of the blessed and great Ganesha Purana in the learned treatise on the immortality of yoga, in the blessed Ganesha Gita which is the essence of the Upanishads.'

Chapter 2

Varenya said, 'Lord, you have declared yoga in knowledge and yoga in activity as being two spiritual paths. After contemplating the two, tell me which one produces the best result.'

Gajanana said, 'In this world of moving and non-moving beings these two were initially declared by me, dear King, in respect to the yoga of the intellect for those of the Sankhya school and the yoga of prescribed actions for those who discharge duties in the world. By not undertaking prescribed actions a man becomes inactive. He gains no success simply by abandoning his duties, King. No one ever remains inactive even for a moment. He is subject to the cosmic forces produced from nature and is compelled to act. But by continually restraining the senses, the man who performs actions remains fixed in consciousness. But because of one's

attachment to sense objects, the fool declares this as stupid behaviour. Having first restrained all of the senses with the mind, he should undertake his duties as the yoga of action by means of the senses. Because he has no material desires, he is superior, King. Action, done without attachment, is superior to no-action. Even the maintenance of the body will not be achieved by inaction. And those who have not offered the results of their actions to Me are bound by them. The imperishable soul should, without attachment, always perform his duties and offer the results to Me. Then any actions performed for Me will never bind one to this world. Action contains unconscious psychic impressions and forcibly binds the embodied soul.

After having produced the social classes, I first explained the sacrifices, dear King. One should continually perpetuate the sacrifices as they satisfy all desires like the wish-fulfilling tree. You must act to please the gods and they will in return please you. By pleasing each other you will permanently obtain the highest goal. The chosen gods, when well-satiated, will give to you your desired corporeal enjoyments. A man who consumes what has been given by the gods, without offering back to them, is a verily a thief. Those who eat the remains of what has been offered as a sacrifice will be freed from all reactions. Those who cook for themselves without offering back to the gods eat selfishly. Beings arise from food. The origin of food is from the gods and the origin of the gods is from the prescribed sacrifices. The prescriptions originate from Brahma and Brahma originates from Me. Hence, Protector of the earth, know that I am present in all sacrifices.

Those who are intelligent will easily cross the ocean of material existence. But the ignorant man who dallies with the senses and happily enjoys them will not. The man who is delighted with the inner self, who rejoices in the self, who enjoys everything, who is satisfied with the self, has no materials desires at all. He does not acquire the good and evil (results) of those who do what should and should not be done. Amongst all men he really accomplishes nothing at all. Therefore, with an attitude of non-attachment, Protector of the Earth, men should undertake action in non-action. One who is attached to the results of his actions, does not obtain the path, but such a man never obtains Me. Previously, sages who were kings and brahmins obtained the highest perfection. So one should undertake such activity for the benefit of all the worlds. Because the prosperous person engages in action, so should every man. Since he considers that the standard, therefore he also should follow that. In the world there is no goal at all that is to be accomplished by Me, Overlord of men. Though I do not need anything that should be gained, I too engage in action. But if, individualistic and prompted by laziness, I do not engage in action, all the social classes will follow my example, Oh intelligent King. Then that world will fall in ruination. I will become known as the destroyer of that world and the cause of collapse of the social classes.

Those who have material desires always perform action ignorantly through desire. The wise man, his mind detached, will act for the benefit of all the worlds. One should not associate with ignorant materialists. Absorbed in yoga, one who engages in action should offer all the results to Me. Absorbed in ignorance with lust, anger and greed as his companions, a person performs actions tirelessly. His intellect contaminated by the ego, he has said, 'I am the doer.' But he who knows the truth of the self, and has conquered his senses and action, is detached, thinking, 'Action has occurred in the field of the senses.'

Those who are infatuated by the senses perform action for a result. The person who has realized the self should not associate with those who are unreceptive towards their own self and who are lacking in faith. Accordingly, the wise man

should offer the continual and occasional results of sacrifice to Me. After giving up the idea of "I" and "mine", he will obtain My Supreme Abode. All those without envy who possess devotion and practice righteous activity, as I have described, are liberated through all their actions.

But those whose minds are dominated by what is inauspicious and do not practice this, know these envious, foolish, ruined people, to be my enemies. In like manner a person who has knowledge engages in activity due to the influence of cosmic nature. However, one who stubbornly engages in activity selfishly is considered to do so in vain. Desire and anger originate in the objects of the senses, but those in knowledge do not work under the influence of either, since they destroy him. One's own dharma whether it is done imperfectly is better than the perfect duty of another. When one stays within one's own duty then liberation is awarded at death. The other produces fear in the other world.'

Varenya said, 'When a man commits evil acts, by what is he urged, even against his own will? Though he may not wish it, Heramba, he is impelled on as if by force.'

The illustrious Gajanana said, 'Anger and desire are huge evils which arise from two of the cosmic strands – passion and ignorance. Both cause bondage in the world. Know them both to be the worst enemies. Just as illusion covers the world, just as steam covers water, just as a rain cloud covers the sun, so do desire and anger cover everything. The intuitive knowledge of one who is in illusion is always covered by hatred, itself filled with desire, energetic, difficult to nourish and impetuous. He exists with the mind and the intellect depending on the pull of the senses. When wisdom is covered by anger and desire, it confuses the person who would otherwise possess intuitive knowledge.

Hence, after first restraining the senses, a man conquers his mind. Evil arises from the mind and brings an end to intuitive and discriminating knowledge. The senses are superior to the intelligence, yet the mind is superior to that. The intellect is superior to the mind and the self is superior to the intellect. After understanding the self by the self and having steadied the self by the self, and after slaying the enemy which takes the form of desire, he attains the highest peace."

Om. This is the truth. This is called 'The Yoga of Action'. It is the second chapter in the conversation between Ganesha and Varenya in the Uttarakhanda of the illustrious and great Ganesha Purana in the learned treatise on the immortality of yoga, in the illustrious Ganesha Gita which is in the essence of the Upanishads.

Chapter 3

The illustrious Ganesha said, 'Formerly, at the time of creation, having produced three bodies relating to creation, maintenance and destruction, I described the supreme yoga to Vishnu. He told it to Aryaman and he to Manu, his own son. From him the great sages knew it as it had come from their lineage. But after a long time, it will be destroyed in the final cosmic period, because it will not be fit for funerary rites, it will not be trusted and will be sung imperfectly, King. You have heard from my mouth this yoga which originated in the past. It is more secret than any secret, it is the secret of the Vedas, supreme and auspicious.'

Varenya said, 'Gajanana, being born into this world, how did you first tell this superb yoga to Vishnu?'

Gajanana said, 'Both you and I have had many past births. I remember them all. You cannot remember any of them. Great-armed king, the gods led by Vishnu, were born from Me alone and after the cosmic destruction, everything is again absorbed in Me alone. I alone am the Supreme Brahman and I alone am the Great Rudra. And I alone am this world and its moving and immovable things. I am unborn, imperishable, the elemental self, having no beginning, the Lord. Though my illusory energy, between the creation, maintenance and destruction of the worlds, I am born within many wombs. When there is an increase in irreligion and a decrease in religion, I am reborn to protect the good and to annihilate the miscreants. Having destroyed the evil ways, I will re-establish true religious principles, and, happily engaging in divine pastimes, I will kill the malevolent and the demons.

Taking many forms I preserve the social classes, the ashrams, and the good. He who knows those divine births of mine millennium after millennium, all my actions, heroic deeds and diviner forms, and gives up the ideas of "I and Mine", he is not reborn in this material world. Without desire, without fear and without anger are they who take refuge in Me, who are absorbed in Me. Many who are purified by austerities in the form of discriminating knowledge have approached me. With whatever form of conviction, those excellent men worship Me, the imperishable, I award them the corresponding result of their devotion. There will be other men, King, who follow my other paths and in that manner alone they conduct their daily business with self-interest and by helping others. Desiring the fruit of their actions they please various deities. In this world they quickly obtain the result that is derived from such acts. From portions of rajas, sattva and tamas and from the portions of the results of past actions, the four social classes were created by Me in the world of mortals. The wise know me as both doer and non-doer, without beginning, the Lord, constant, untouched by the qualities which arise from actions.

Karma certainly does not bind him who knows the absence of desire. Having first understood this, those who want liberation perform action. Understanding this, a man is freed from all bondage to ignorance that is certainly caused by connection with the psychic traces from earlier actions, from what is eaten, and by transmigration in the world. Hence I will now tell you about action and non-action, in respect of which the sages who have understanding become free from delusion.

The truth of action and non-action are realized by a person who seeks liberation. The path of those who are profound comprises three kinds of actions in the world, dear one. Whoever has knowledge of inaction in action and the understanding of action in inaction, will be liberated in this mortal world while performing all his actions. Without the fruition of past actions what man would begin any actions. The wise declare the intelligent man as one whose actions are consumed by a vision of the truth. After giving up the desire for results of one's present activities, he will always be satisfied, even without striving. Though ready to undertake activity, he does nothing at all. Without desire, self-controlled, given up possessiveness, doing only those duties required for his maintenance, he does not fall from his position. Having adopted the view that there are no opposites, being without greed and having the same attitude towards success and failure, very happy in the world because he has attained such a state, he engages in activity and is not bound. He who possesses intuitive and discriminating knowledge is freed from all sense-objects. All the karmic results of activity he engages in for the sake of sacrifice is destroyed.

Thinking, 'I am fire, the oblation, the offered, the burnt offering and I am offered to You,' he should realize Brahman, since he is devoted to Brahman alone. Some yogis speak that karmic destiny is the sacrifice. Others think that the fire of Brahman is the sacrifice. Others offer the senses into the fire of restraint, Protector of the earth. Others offer the sense objects, sound etc., into the fires of the sense organs. Others offer the actions of their vital breaths and sense organs in the fire of the joy of their own Self-kindled with knowledge or with the austerity as the substance of recitation of the sacred texts to oneself.

Ascetics sacrifice to Me with severe vows and knowledge. They cast their outgoing breath into their incoming breath and their incoming breath into their outgoing breath. And after suppressing the movements of both, they focus on restraint of the breath. Once he has conquered the breaths, he offers the movements of the breath into them. In this way, devoted to various sacrifices, their evil actions are destroyed by the sacrifice. Those who eat the nectar of the remains of the sacrifice proceed to the eternal Brahman. This world is not for the man who does not sacrifice. Whence where will there be another world for him? By knowing, Protector of the Earth, that all these sacrifices, which are of three kinds – pertaining to the body and the rest, are grounded in the Vedas, you will become free of any attachment.

Of all sacrifices, the sacrifice of knowledge is considered the best. All results of actions are dissolved in knowledge that leads to liberation. True knowledge, O tiger of men, can be known by humbly questioning and serving the self-realized soul. Those who are enlightened will speak only truth. A man who, due to many attachments, does not hear from self-realized soul, will, in consequence, act in the world of transmigration and enter material bondage. Through attachment to the good soul there arises good qualities and the disappearance of misfortunes. This sort of good fortune is gained in this world and in the next. Material fortune is easy to obtain, King, but association with the good soul is difficult to find. Once he knows what should be known he is not reborn here or there. Then he sees all beings as his own self, that same man intent upon committing sin is freed from even that.

Different kinds of actions are instantly burnt in the fire of knowledge. Just as a fire that has been started does not instantly turn everything to ashes, other purifications, King, are not identical with knowledge. In time yogis realize the self through yoga. The devotee who conquers the senses and concentrates the mind on the Self, he will obtain divine knowledge. After gaining That, which is Supreme, he becomes liberated after a short time. But the person who has no devotion, who has no faith and always doubts, he has no discriminating knowledge that is a refuge here or in other worlds. There are those who the results of actions have been destroyed by yoga, who are intent upon knowledge of the self, and whose doubts are destroyed through knowledge. These actions do not bind. Therefore, having forcibly cut the doubts in the heart, which have arisen by ignorance, by the sword of knowledge, a man should stay fixed in

yoga."

Om. This is the truth. This is called 'The Attainment of Knowledge'. It is the third chapter in the conversation between Ganesha and Varenya in the Uttarakhanda of the illustrious and great Ganesha Purana in the learned treatise on the immortality of yoga, in the illustrious Ganesha Gita which is in the essence of the Upanishads.

Chapter 4

Varenya said, 'You have described renunciation and the yoga of action. But of these two, tell me Lord, which one is certainly the best.

Gajanana said, 'The yoga of action and the renunciation of action are both practices for liberation. Between these two the yoga of action is distinguished from the renunciation of action. That person who is not affected by duality, who does not hate and desires nothing, renounces and is instantly and easily freed from bondage. They say that the acceptance of action and the renunciation of action have two different results. With just incomplete knowledge influenced by attraction for that yoga, the wise man attaches himself to one. Whatever is gained by renouncing the result of action is the fruit of yoga. Whoever knows this yoga as the acceptance of action, knows truly.

Only the wise know that renunciation is not the abandonment of action. The yogi in action who acts without desire becomes situated in Brahman. Pure, with his self and mind restrained, his senses conquered, he is completely absorbed in yoga. Whilst seeing the self in all beings, he acts without being tainted. The one who knows the truth and whose self is controlled by yoga, does not think, 'I am acting'. They regard the eleven senses as the enumeration of actions. He who acts should offer all actions to God and is not tainted by evil or merit, in the same way as the light of the sun, which moves, truly is not affected by which it touches. After giving up desire – pertaining to the body, speech, intellect, the senses and the mind – for the purification of consciousness, those who know yoga perform actions. One who is not situated in yoga who simply desires the fruits of action, is bound by the seeds of action. This eventually becomes one's unhappiness.

After mentally renouncing all action within the mind the yogi becomes happy. Neither acting for his own enjoyment, nor causing others to act in the same way, he rejoices in any condition either good or bad. Neither action nor the vehicle of action is created for anyone by Me. There is no interference and every action is done automatically through My energy. King, I do not cause the good or evil reactions for anyone. Those who have a poor fund of knowledge, their intellect covered by maya, are perplexed. Of those whose ignorance is destroyed by the self through discrimination of the self, their excellent knowledge shines like the sun. Those who are absorbed in Me, those whose minds definitely rest in

Me, whose thoughts are on Me, who are fixed on Me, having discriminating knowledge, they are not reborn, their karmas destroyed. Those great munis who see with equal vision a dog, a dog eater, cows and elephants and all living creatures, and a brahmin who has discriminating and intuitive knowledge, always experiences the world as heaven. Seeing all equally, they are liberated whilst alive. Since Brahman is pure and equal, It is therefore perceived by them. After having experienced what is considered pleasant or unpleasant, they are neither elated nor distained. Resting in Brahman, in full knowledge, they know Brahman, regarding all things as the same spirit.

Varenya said, 'What happiness is there in the three worlds when one is born as a demigod or a heavenly musician? Kindly, tell me Lord, as you are skilled in all knowledge.'

Ganesha said, 'The man who delights in his own self and is attached to his own self, attains bliss and eternal happiness, for there is no happiness in the realm of the senses. Enjoyments which arise from the objects of the senses are the causes of misery and are connected to birth and death. The wise man is not attached to them. Given that desire and anger have a cause, he is able to conquer them by leaving aside worldly aspirations and he thus attains lasting happiness. Absorbed in the soul, emanating in the soul, happy in the soul, he who delights in the soul, and is the well-wisher of all living beings, will certainly gain the imperishable Brahman. They conquer the six enemies and are tranquil and controlled.

Listen! For those who know their own self Brahman emanates everywhere. Seated in yogic asanas having controlled the mind through detachment from the objects of the senses. After concentrating the mind in the centre of the brow, he sits, focused on breath control, which is the suspension of the inward breath. The insightful sages declare it to be of three kinds. Understand the division to be of weak, middle and highest standard. Pranayama is said to be the weakest because it has twelve vowels. It is declared to be middle because it has twenty-one vowels. It is declared to be at the highest standard when it has thirty-six light vowels. Just like a lion or a tiger is compared to a furious elephant in weakness, so are ordinary living beings compared to the yogi. A person should control outward breath and the inward breath. One does not hurt animals nor people who have come under their auspices, King, just as air which is controlled burns away one's karma, but not one's body.

In whatever way a man might climb the stairs, so the yogis will bring the breath and the downward-moving-breath under control. After that the man should practice the drawing up of air, the stopping of breath and breathing out through one nostril. After that he will become one with the world and will know the past and the future. The concentration of the mind is considered to be the result of the excellent twelve-vowel exercise of hatha yoga.

There is yoga that encompasses two acts of concentration. The master of yoga should always practice one. Whoever does this, lord, comes to know the three worlds. The triple-world will effortlessly come under his control, king. He sees the world in his own self under the form of Brahman. In this way yogic asanas or renunciation of action give the same result to the person who does good for people and is not attached to the results of his action. After he knows Me as the mighty Lord of the triple-world, he gains liberation.

Om. This is the truth. This is called 'The Two-fold Yoga and Renunciation'. It is the fourth chapter in the conversation between Ganesha and Varenya in the Uttarakhanda of the illustrious and great Ganesha Purana in the learned treatise on the immortality of yoga, in the illustrious Ganesha Gita which is in the essence of the Upanishads.

Chapter 5

Gajanana said, 'My dear King, not desiring the results of one's activities, whether they be termed transcendent or ritualistic, the yogi is recommended to perform his duties, not by ceasing action, but from a reliance on yoga. Mighty-armed King, I consider that devotional service alone is the cause for attaining yoga. Peacefulness and restraining the senses are considered the causes for success in siddha-yoga. Focusing on the objects of the senses is considered the enemy of oneself. The yogi who ignores the craving of the senses gains success. One's own self exists only through the self. We do not exist as separate from the self. Whether in friendship, or enmity, in freedom or imprisonment, in honour, disgrace, unhappiness and happiness, or with a close friend or amongst the good, in a friend, in an enemy, in indifference and hatred, sees iron and gold, the person who has conquered the self, who has discriminating knowledge, intuitive knowledge and continually has control over the senses, maintains the same equanimity. He becomes highly controlled when he practices yoga continually. Whether he is distressed, exhausted, confused, hungry, agitated in his thoughts, whether in time, in excessive cold, excessive heat or a mass of wind, fire and water, when quiet, very old, in a cow pen, in fire, near water, in a pool or in a hole, in a cemetery, on the bank of a river, near an old wall, near a funeral monument which has an anthill, in a country abounding in demons, etc., the knower of yoga, who is dedicated to meditation and yoga, should not practice yoga in inaction alone.

Forgetfulness, being dumb, deaf, drunk, feverish and stupid always occur. They are flaws that arise through separation from knowledge. These flaws must be completely eradicated by one who habitually practices yoga, because a lack of diligence in respect of yogic practice, loss of memory and the rest certainly occur. The yogi, never eating too much, but not eating too little, does not sleep excessively, nor does he remain awake to excess. He achieves success, Protector of the Earth, always practicing yoga. He should give up intentional desires and when restrained in eating and sleeping, after controlling all the senses, he should slowly withdraw the senses by means of the intelligence. He should withdrawal the fickle consciousness away from whatever it dwells on and, after concentrating the mind, he should diligently bring it under control of the self. Doing this always, the yogi attains the highest bliss and perceives his own self in everything and everything in his own self.

Whoever approaches Me through yoga, I respectfully approach him also. I will liberate him, yet he should never abandon Me or I cannot free him. A person who has the same attitude in happiness, pain, exaltation, hatred, satiation and in thirst knows Me as omnipresent and knows all beings through the identity of the self. Liberated whilst alive, he is the lord of yogi's because he is only attached to Me. And he will be praised by the demigods led by Brahma.

Varenya said, 'I think this yoga must be considered as having two kinds, since the mind is bad, fickle and difficult to hold, Lord.'

The illustrious Gajanana said, 'Whoever restrains the mind, which is difficult to control, is liberated from the wheel of existence which is like a machine for raising water. I created the solid wheel with saws which are the sense objects. A man cannot split it when it is completely covered by the spokes of karma. Austerity, dispassion, absence of desire in regard to corporeal enjoyments, the blessings of a guru, association with the good: these are the instruments for victory over samsara. Or, through yoga, he should bring the mind under control for its success. Varenya, this yoga is difficult to gain without victory over the mind.'

Varenya said, 'What is the world for a man who has fallen away from yoga? What is his opinion and what will the result be? Lord, you are omniscient, so resolve this doubt which carries with it the wheel as the intellect.'

The illustrious Gajanana said, 'A man who has a celestial body and has fallen away from yoga after he has enjoyed superb enjoyments in heaven, will be born in the family of a yogi, in the family of those who are pure. This yogi is reborn again due to the mental formations produced by prior karma, for one who has accumulated merit never reaches hell. By being fixed in knowledge, fixed in intellect, fixed in austerities and fixed in right action, overlord of men, he becomes the best yogi. Amongst them, the very best is the yogi who is devoted to Me.'

Om. This is the truth. This is called 'The Yoga which concerns the Application of Yoga'. It is the fifth chapter in the conversation between Ganesha and Varenya in the Uttarakhanda of the illustrious and great Ganesha Purana in the learned treatise on the immortality of yoga, in the illustrious Ganesha Gita which is in the essence of the Upanishads.

CHAPTER 3

LORD GANESHA IN MUDGALA PURANA

3.1 Introduction to Mudgala Purana

The Mudgala Purana (mudgala purāṇam) is a Hindu religious text dedicated to the Hindu deity Ganesha (Gaṇeśa). It is an upapurāṇa that includes many stories and ritualistic elements relating to Ganesha. The Ganesha Purana and the Mudgala Purana are the core scriptures for devotees of Ganesha, known as Ganapatyas (Gāṇapatya). These are the only two Purana that are exclusively dedicated to Ganesha.

Like the Ganesha Purana, the Mudgala Purana considers Ganesha to represent the ultimate reality of being. As such, Ganesha's manifestations are endless but eight of his incarnations (avatāra) are of most importance. The text is organized into sections for each of these incarnations. These are not the same as the four incarnations of Ganesha that are described in the Ganesha Purana.

3.2 Eight Incarnations (Avatars) of Lord Ganesha

Ganesha took eight avatars or incarnations to save the world from demons who personified a dosha or shortcoming in human nature? These doshas are also present in gods and it is through them that the demons were born. The incarnation described in the Mudgala Purana took place in different cosmic ages. The Mudgala Purana uses these incarnations to express complex philosophical concepts associated with the progressive creation of the world. Each incarnation represents a stage of the absolute as it unfolds into creation.

The incarnations appear in the following order:

(i) **Vakratunda (Vakratuṇḍa) ("twisting trunk"),** first in the series, represents the absolute as the aggregate of all bodies, an embodiment of the form of Brahman. The purpose of this incarnation is to overcome the demon Matsaryāsura (envy, jealousy). His mount (vāhana) is a lion.

According to the legend, Lord Indra's pramaada (heedlessness) gave birth to the demon Matsarasura. Matsara means jealousy and selfishness. After severe penance, Matsarasura received the boon of fearlessness from Shiva. He along with his two sons Sundarpriya and Vishaypriya, conquered the three worlds and created havoc everywhere. All the gods approached Shiva for help but bound by his own boon, Shiva could not do much. Finally, Lord Dattatreya came to the rescue. He gave all the gods the secret of the monosyllabic mantra, Gam, and asked them to call upon Lord Vakratunda. Seated on his vehicle, the lion, Vakratunda arrived and killed both sons of Matsara. Looking at the mighty god, the demon surrendered and asked for forgiveness. The

Lord forgave him and restored the three worlds. Ganesha, in his Vakratunda avatar, shows the world that however powerful or rich you are, wisdom lies in knowing and understanding your limits.

> **(ii) Ekadanta ("single tusk"),** represents the aggregate of all individual souls, an embodiment of the essential nature of Brahman. the purpose of this incarnation is to overcome the demon Madāsura (arrogance, conceit). His mount is a mouse.

The asura, Chyavana, had a son, Mada, who was fond of madira or alcohol. Mada was schooled by his uncle Shukracharya, Chyavana's brother as well as the guru of the asuras. Madasura told Shukracharya that he wanted to rule the world. Pleased by his nephew's ambition, Shukracharya gave him the Shakti Mantra 'Hrim'. Madasura performed penance for a thousand years invoking the goddess and received special powers from her. Armed with these new powers, and high on alcohol and arrogance, Madasura started conquering the three worlds. The gods turned to the sage, Sanat Kumara, for help. Sanat Kumara asked them to invoke Ekadanta. Seated on Mooshika, Ekadanta came to wage war against the demon. However, Madasura lost his courage in front of the mighty god and surrendered, earning Ekadanta's forgiveness. Ganesha in Ekadanta avatar shows us that intoxication can fill one with pride beyond control.

(iii) Mahodara ("big belly"), is a synthesis of both Vakratuṇḍa and Ekadanta. It is the absolute as it enters into the creative process. It is an embodiment of the wisdom of Brahman. The purpose of this incarnation is to overcome the demon Mohāsura (delusion, confusion). is mount is a mouse.

The story of Ganesha's third avatar, Mahodara, has two versions. The first version talks of the main antagonist, Mohasura, who came to be known as Daitya Raj or the king of the asuras, because of his devotion to Surya, the sun god. In the second version, once when Shiva was in deep meditation and the gods needed him, they asked Parvati to help break his trance. Parvati took an alluring form and distracted Shiva. When Shiva came out of his meditative state, Parvati discarded her alluring form. This discarded energy took the form of Mohasura, the embodiment of delusion, who then went on a rampage against all three worlds. Both stories conclude similarly. The terrified gods went to Surya for help. Surya advised them to pray to Mahodara. Pleased by the prayers, Mahodara arrives on Mooshika to wage war against Mohasura. At this point, Vishnu appears, advising Mohasura to surrender, as all would be forgiven. Mohasura pays heed to Lord Vishnu's advice and surrenders himself to Mahodara, becoming his devotee forever.

(iv) Gajavaktra (or Gajānana) ("elephant face"), is a counterpart to Mahodara. The purpose of this incarnation is to overcome the demon Lobhāsura (greed). His mount is a mouse.

Kubera, the treasurer of the heavens, once visited Kailasha, the abode of Lord Shiva. He looked at goddess Parvati with lustful eyes, which made the goddess angry. Kubera started shivering with fear. This fearful energy got manifested into Lobha. Lobhasura went on to study under Shukracharya, using the mantra 'Om Namah Shivaya' to perform penance, and eventually gain enough power to conquer the three realms. Troubled, the gods approached sage Raibhya who told them to pray to Lord Gajanana. The sheer presence of Gajanana was enough to fill Lobhasura with guilt, who begs for forgiveness. This avatar shows the world that lust is self-indulgent and self-centred and unknowingly leads to the destruction of the soul.

(v) Lambodara ("pendulous belly"), is the first of four incarnations that correspond to the stage where the Purāṇic gods are created. Lambodara corresponds to Shakti, the pure power of Brahman. The purpose of this incarnation is to overcome the demon Krodhāsura (anger). His mount is a mouse.

During the episode of the celestial churning of the ocean, Vishnu took the form of the beautiful and charming Mohini to trick the asuras. However, he did not see

Shiva becoming enchanted by this avatar of his. When he realizes this, Vishnu immediately reverts to his original form. This made Shiva sad and angry and this anger manifested into a terrible demon named Krodhasura. Krodhasura became Shukracharya's student, venerating the Sun god and performed penance, becoming powerful enough to - you guessed it - wreak havoc on the three worlds. To stop Krodhasura's rampage, Ganesha took the form of Lambodara and appeared with a potbelly large enough to accommodate the anger of the demon Krodhasura! Lambodara manages to subdue Krodhasura and peace is restored.

(vi) Vikata (Vikaṭa) ("unusual form", "misshapen"), corresponds to Sūrya. He is an embodiment of the illuminating nature of Brahman. The purpose of this incarnation is to overcome the demon Kāmāsura (lust). His mount is a peacock.

Kamasura was born of Vishnu and Vrinda, the wife of the demon Jalandhara. He embodied trickery, lust and the consequences of lust. Kamasura took refuge with Shukracharya, the guru of the asuras and was told to observe severe penance and meditate on Shiva. Kamasura then received a boon by which he conquered the three worlds and created trouble for all the gods. On the sage Mudgala's advice, the gods begin to chant 'Om' in a place called Mayuresa Kshetra, thus summoning Ganesha in the avatar of Vikata, atop a peacock. In his Vikata avatar, Ganesha is able to easily defeat Kamasura. This avatar shows the world that desire has no end. Satisfaction and happiness are not the outcomes of any achievement but a state of being that comes from within.

(vii) Vighnaraja (Vighnarāja) ("king of obstacles"), corresponds to Viṣṇu. He is an embodiment of the preserving nature of Brahman. The purpose of this incarnation is to overcome the demon Mamāsura (possessiveness). His mount is the celestial serpent Shesha.

Once, goddess Parvati was relaxing in the company of her friends in a forest when her burst of laughter manifested into a handsome boy. Surprised by her creation and swayed by her ego which resulted in attachment, she named him 'Mama' which in Sanskrit means 'Mine'. She told him to always follow the right path and pray to Lord Ganesha. Mama decides to retire to the forests to meditate on Lord Ganesha but meets the demon Sambara on the way. Sambara lures him into the world of the asuras and slowly, the good-natured Mama becomes the demon Mamasura. He marries Mohini, the daughter of an asura chief, and starts his campaign to rule all three worlds. Defeated and thrown out of Swarga loka, the gods turn to Ganesha for help. So he takes on the avatar of Vighnaraja - the remover of obstacles. Riding on the great serpent, Sheshnaaga, Vighnaraja tames the demon of attachment and restores peace. Vignhnaraja was a symbol that showed the world that there is no pleasure in worldly attachments. The soul seeks truth and divinity, everything else is an illusion.

> **(viii) Dhumravarna (Dhūmravarṇa) ("grey colour")**, corresponds to Shiva. He is an embodiment of the destructive nature of Brahman. The purpose of this incarnation is to overcome the demon Abhimanāsura (pride, attachment). His mount is a mouse.

This was the last avatar of Ganesha's. Once Brahma gave the right to rule over the 'world of action' to his grandson, the sun god Surya. Surya grew proud and thought to himself that since the entire world is governed by karma or action, he had become the lord of the whole world. As this thought passed his mind, he happened to sneeze and from his sneeze manifested a demon. The demon went to Shukracharya who gave him the name Ahamkarasura, as he was born from the sun's ego. Shukracharya also asked him to do penance and meditate on Ganesha. Terrified by Ahamkaura's growing power, the gods look to Ganesha for help. Ganesha obliged, taking on the form of Dhumravarna, arriving on Mooshika and defeating the proud demon. This episode reminds us that 'ahamkar' or ego is the root cause of self-destruction.

3.3 History of Mudgala Purana

There is little agreement on the date of the Mudgala Purana. The Mudgala was the last of the philosophical texts concerned with Ganesha. According to another report, the Mudgala Purana is earlier than the Ganesha Purana which dates between 1100 and 1400 A.D. The Mudgala Purana specifically mentions the Ganesha

Purana as one of the four Puranas that deal at length with Ganesha. These are the Brahma, the Brahmaṇḍa, the Ganesha, and the Mudgala puranas. Different views on the relative dating of these two works conclude that the Mudgala Purana, like other Puranas, is a multi-laid work. The kernel of the text must be old and that it must have continued to receive interpolations until the 17th and 18th centuries as the worship of Ganapati became more important in certain regions.

CHAPTER 4

LORD GANESHA IN GANAPATI ATHARVASHIRSHA PURANA (GANAPATI UPANISHAD)

4.1 Ganapati Atharvashirsha Purana (Ganapati Upanishad)

The Ganapati Atharvasirsha (Gaṇapatyatharvaśīrṣa) is a Sanskrit text and a minor Upanishad of Hinduism. It is a late Upanishadic text dedicated to Ganesha, the deity representing intellect and learning. It asserts that Ganesha is same as the eternal underlying reality, Brahman. The text is attached to the Atharvaveda, and is also referred to as the Sri Ganapati Atharva Sirsha, the Ganapati Atharvashirsha, the Ganapati Atharvasirsa, or the Ganapati Upanishad.

The text exists in several variants, but with the same message. Ganesha is described to be same as other Hindu gods, as ultimate truth and reality (Brahman), as satchidananda, as the soul in oneself (Atman) and in every living being, as Om.

The text identifies Ganesha with the Brahman and is of a very late origin, it is dated to the 16th or 17th century. While the Upanishad is a late text, the earliest mention of the word Ganapati is found in hymn 2.23.1 of the 2nd-millennium BCE Rigveda. Ganapati literally means "leader of the multitudes", it is however uncertain that the Vedic term referred specifically to Ganesha.

The Ganapati Upanishad text is listed at number 89 in the Muktikā canon of 108 Upanishads compiled in the mid-17th century, and also mentioned c. 1800 by Upanishad Brahmayogin in his commentary on the Muktika canon.

4.2 Ganesha as the Supreme Reality

The first verse of the Upanishad proper asserts that Ganesha is the Supreme principle and all-pervading metaphysical absolute reality called Brahman in Hinduism. Ganesha is asserted by the text as identical to Om, the Brahman, the Atman or soul, and as the visible manifestation of the Vedic idea: 'Tat tvam asi (you are that)', found in the sixth chapter of the Chandogya Upanishad, in a manner similar to Shiva in Shaiva Upanishads, Vishnu in Vaishnava Upanishads, and Devi in Shakti Upanishads.

Homage to Lord Ganesha. Oṃ. Reverence to Gaṇapati. You are indeed the visible "That Thou Art" [tattvamasi]. You indeed produce the universe. You indeed sustain it. You indeed destroy it. You indeed are the all-pervading reality. You are the manifestation of the eternal self (Brahman).

This verse is translated as follows:

(O Lord Ganapati!) You alone are the visible manifestation of the Essence of the words "That thou art". You alone are the Doer. You alone are the Creator and the Sustainer (of the universe). You alone are the Destroyer. Verily You alone are all this - "idam sarvam" - in the creation, because You are Brahman. You are the Eternal Atman in bodily form."

4.3 Identification of Ganesha with other Deities and with Om

Ganesha is same as Brahma, Vishnu, Shiva, all deities, the universe and the Om. Ganesha, asserts the text, is the Absolute, as well the same soul is each of every living being.

You are Brahmā, Vishu, and Rudra [Shiva]. You are Agni, Vāyu, and Sūrya. You are Chandrama. You are earth, space, and heaven. You are the manifestation of the mantra "Oṃ".

A variant version of this passage is translated as follows:

(O Lord Ganapati!) You are (the Trinity) Brahma, Vishnu, and Mahesha. You are Indra. You are fire and air. You are the sun and the moon. You are Brahman. You are (the three worlds) Bhuloka, Antariksha-loka, and Swargaloka. You are Om. (that is to say, You are all this).

The verses state Ganesha to be all that is spiritual, the satchidananda, all words, all four levels of speech, all knowledge, all consciousness, the source of all universe, the universe now, that in which the universe will someday be dissolved, the three Guṇas of Samkhya philosophy and what is beyond, all states of being, the truth, the oneness, the contentment, the inner bliss.

4.4 Integration of Tantra

Some evidence that the work is of late origin which associate Ganapati with the Muladhara chakra:

Tvam Muladharasthititoasi nityam.

Meaning: You continually dwell in the muladhara chakra.

This text provides a detailed description of Ganesha's bija mantra gam. When this mantra is written using simplified transliteration methods that do not include diacritical marks to represent nasal sounds, it is written as "gam". This bija mantra is also used in the Ganesha Purana which is generally dated as preceding the Ganapati Atharvasirsa.

This passage is translated as follows (Ganesha Gayatri):

Ekadantaya vidyamhe

Vsakratundaya dhimahi

Tanno dantih Prachodayat.

Meaning: May we know the single tusked one,

May we meditate on the one with the curved trunk,

May that tusked one inspire knowledge and meditation of ours.

—Ganapati Upanishad 8,

Having uttered the first letter of the word gaṇa, 'ga', then I utter the nasal sound 'ṇa' which follows and appears beautifully like the crescent moon. This is your form. The 'ga' forms the initial letter, the 'a' forms the middle letter and the 'ṇa' forms the final letter. To utter this sound [i.e., gaṃ] is to utter all sounds together.

4.5 Ganesha Gayatri Mantra

The text includes a Gayatri mantra in verse 8, with Ganesha as the source of inspiration for meditation and knowledge, in Nrichad Gayatri poetic meter. This distills the highest human spiritual aspiration. The tooth and trunk in the Ganesha-Gayatri mantra embodies symbolism for philosophical and spiritual truths, channeling the attention to physical, intellectual and intuitional self-realization.

4.6 Colophon (a publisher's emblem or imprint)

The text asserts its own status as an Upanishad in its final line, which reads "Thus, the Śrī Gaṇapati Atharvaśīrṣa Upanishad"; śrīgaṇapatyatharvaśīrṣopaniṣad). The text associates itself with the Atharvaveda, in a passage that translates as "Thus says Atharvana".

The text ends with the Shanti hymn, states Grimes, "May we be protected together, may we be sustained together, may we do great deeds together, Om, peace, peace, peace!".

4.7 Reception and Reverence of Ganapati

It is the most important surviving Sanskrit text in the Ganapatyas tradition of Hinduism, wherein Ganesha is revered. The entire text is written over the entrance to the temple hall in the aṣtavināyaka Ganesha shrine at Ranjangaon.

4.8 Complete Text of Ganapati Upanishad

Om Namas-Te Gannapataye (1)

1. Om Gam. I bow to Ganapati.

Tvam-Eva Pratyakssam Tattvam-Asi |

Tvam-Eva Kevalam Kartaa-[A]si |

Tvam-Eva Kevalam Dhartaa-[A]si |

Tvam-Eva Kevalam Hartaa-[A]si |

Tvam-Eva Sarvam Khalv[u]-Idam Brahma-Asi |

Tvam Saakssaad-Aatmaa-[A]si Nityam ||2||

2. You clearly are the tattva. You alone are the creator. You alone are the maintainer. You alone are the destroyer. Of all this you certainly are Brahman. You plainly are the essence.

Rtam Vacmi | Satyam Vacmi ||3||

3. Always I speak amrta. The truth I speak.

Ava Purastaat |

Ava Dakssinnaattaat |

Ava Pashcaattaat |

Avo[a-U]ttaraattaat |

Ava Co[a-U]rdhvaattaat |

Ava-Adharaattaat |

Sarvato Maam Paahi Paahi Samantaat ||4||

4. Protect me. Protect the speakers. Protect the hearers. Protect the givers. Protect the holders. Protect the disciple that repeats. Protect that in the east. Protect that in the south. Protect that in the west. Protect that in the north. Protect that above. Protect that below. Everywhere protect! Protect me everywhere!

Tvam Vaangmayas-Tvam Cinmayah |

Tvam-Aanandamayas-Tvam Brahmamayah |

Tvam Saccidaanandaa-[A]dvitiiyo-[A]si |

Tvam Pratyakssam Brahma-Asi |

Tvam Jnyaanamayo Vijnyaanamayo-[A]si ||5||

5. You are speech. You are consciousness. You are bliss. You are Brahman. You are being consciousness-bliss. You are the non-dual. You are plainly Brahman. You are knowledge. You are intelligence.

Tvam Brahmaa Tvam Vissnnus-Tvam

Rudras-Tvam-Indras-Tvam-Agnis-Tvam

Vaayus-Tvam Suuryas-Tvam Candramaas-Tvam

Brahma Bhuur-Bhuvas-Suvar-Om ||6||

6. You create all this world. You maintain all this world. All this world is seen in you. You are earth, water, air, fire, ether. You are beyond the four measures of speech. You are beyond the three gunas. You are beyond the three bodies. You are beyond the three times. You are always situated in the muladhara. You are the being of the three Shaktis. You are always meditated on by yogins. You are Brahma, you are Vishnu, you are Rudra, you are Agni, you are Vayu, you are the sun, you are the moon, you are Brahma, bhur-bhuvah-svar.

Ganna-[A]adim Puurvam-Uccaarya Varnna-[A]adiims-Tad-Anantaram |

Anusvaarah Paratarah |

Ardhendu-Lasitam |

Taarenna Rddham |

Etat-Tava Manu-Svaruupam ||7||

7. 'Ga' is the first syllable, after that the first letter, beyond that 'm', then the half-moon all together. Joined with 'm', this is the mantra form (Gam).

Ga-kaarah Puurva-Ruupam |

A-kaaro Madhya-Ruupam |

Anusvaarash-Ca-Antya-Ruupam |

Bindur-Uttara-Ruupam |

Naadas-Samdhaanam |

Samhitaa Samdhih ||8||

8. The letter 'ga' is the first form, letter 'a' the middle form, 'm' the last form. Bindu the higher form, nada the joining together, samhita the junction. This is the vidya of Lord Ganesha.

Sai[a-E]ssaa Gannesha-Vidyaa |

Gannaka Rssih |

Nicrdgaayatriic-Chandah |

Gannapatir-Devataa |

Om Gam Gannapataye Namah ||9||

9. Ganaka is the seer, nricad-gayatri the metre, Sri Mahaganapati the devata. Om ganapataye namah.

Eka-Dantaaya Vidmahe Vakra-Tunnddaaya Dhiimahi |

Tan-No Dantih Pracodayaat ||10||

10. Let us think of the one-toothed, let us meditate on the crooked trunk, may that tusk direct us.

Eka-Dantam Catur-Hastam Paasham-Angkusha-
Dhaarinnam |

Radam Ca Vara-Dam Hastair-Bibhraannam Muussaka-
Dhvajam ||

Raktam Lambo[a-U]daram Shuurpa-Karnnakam Rakta-
Vaasasam |

Rakta-Gandha-Anulipta-Anggam Rakta-Pusspais-
Supuujitam ||11||

11. One tusk, four arms, carrying noose and goad, with his hands dispelling fear and granting boons, with a mouse as his banner.

Namo Vraata-Pataye |

Namo Ganna-Pataye |

Namah Pramatha-Pataye |

Namas-Te-[A]stu Lambo[a-U]daraayai[a-E]ka-Dantaaya

Vighna-Naashine Shiva-Sutaaya Varada-Muurtaye
Namah ||12||

12. Red, with a big belly, with ears like winnowing baskets, wearing red, with limbs smeared with red scent, truly worshipped with red flowers.

Saayam-Adhiiyaano Divasa-Krtam Paapam Naashayati |

Praatar-Adhiiyaano Raatri-Krtam Paapam Naashayati |

Saayam Praatah Prayun.jaano Paapo-[A]paapo Bhavati |

Sarvatra-Adhiiyaano-[A]pavighno Bhavati |

Dharma-Artha-Kaama-Mokssam Ca Vindati ||13||

13. To the devoted a merciful deva, the maker of the world, the prime cause, who at the beginning of creation was greater than nature and man.

Bhakta-Anukampinam Devam Jagat-Kaarannam-
Acyutam |

Aavirbhuutam Ca Srssttya[i-A]adau Prakrteh
Purussaat-Param |

Evam Dhyaayati Yo Nityam Sa Yogii Yoginaam Varah
||14||

14. He who always meditates thus is a yogin above yogins.

Anena Gannapatim-Abhissin.cati Sa Vaagmii Bhavati |

Caturthyaam-Anashnan Japati Sa Vidyaavaan Bhavati |

Itya[i-A]tharvanna-Vaakyam |

*Brahma-Adya-[A]avarannam Vidyaan-Na Bibheti
Kadaacane[a-I]ti ||15||*

15. Hail to the lord of vows, hail to Ganapati, hail to the first lord, hail unto you, to the big-bellied, one-tusked, obstacle-destroyer, the son of Siva, to the boon-giver, hail, hail!

*Yo Duurvaa-[A]ngkurair-Yajati Sa Vaishravanno[a-U]
pamo Bhavati |*

Yo Laajair-Yajati Sa Yashovaan Bhavati |

Sa Medhaavaan Bhavati |

*Yo Modaka-Sahasrenna Yajati Sa Vaan.chita-Phalam-
Avaapnoti |*

*Yas-Saajya-Samidbhir-Yajati Sa Sarvam Labhate Sa
Sarvam Labhate ||16||*

16. He who studies this atharva text moves towards Brahma. He is always blissful. He is not bound by any obstacles. He is liberated from the five greater and the five lesser sins. Evening meditation destroys the unmeritorious actions of the night. At both evening and morning he

is liberated from the bad and he attains dharma, artha, kama and moksha.

Idam-Atharvashiirssam-Ashissyaaya Na Deyam |

Yo Yadi Mohaad-Daasyati Sa Paapiiyaan Bhavati |

Sahasra-[A]avartanaad-Yam Yam Kaamam-Adhiite Tam Tam-Anena Saadhayet ||17||

17. This atharva text should not be given to those not pupils. If from delusion a person so gives, he is a bad person.

Assttau Braahmannaan Samyag Graahayitvaa Suurya-Varcasvii Bhavati |

Suuryagrahe-Mahaa-Nadyaam Pratimaa-Sannidhau Vaa Japtvaa Siddha-Mantro Bhavati

Mahaa-Vighnaat Pramucyate |

Mahaa-Dossaat Pramucyate |

Mahaa-Pratyavaayaat Pramucyate |

Sa Sarvavid Bhavati Sa Sarva-Vid Bhavati |

Ya Evam Veda |

Ity[i]-Upanissat ||18||

18. He who wants something may accomplish it by 1,000 recitations of this. He who sprinkles Ganapati with this becomes eloquent. He who recites this on a fourth day becomes a knower of vidya. This is an artharva saying: "He who moves towards Brahmavidya is never afraid." He who worships with fried grains becomes famous and

becomes intelligent. He who worships with sweet-meat (modaka) gains the desired fruit. He who worships with samit and ghee by him all is attained, all is gained by him. He who makes eight brahmnas understand this becomes like the sun's rays. In a solar eclipse, in a great river, or in front of an image having recited (this) he gets accomplished in the mantra. He becomes liberated from great obstacles. He is freed from great misfortunes.

CHAPTER 5

LORD GANESHA IN SKANDA PURANA

5.1 Introduction to Skanda Purana

The Skanda Purana is the largest Mahāpurāṇa, a genre of eighteen Hindu religious texts. The text contains over 81,000 verses, and is of Kaumara literature, titled after Skanda (Kandhan), a son of Shiva and Parvati, who is also known as Murugan. While the text is named after Skanda, he does not feature either more or less prominently in this text than in other Shiva-related Puranas. The text has been an important historical record and influence on the Hindu traditions related to the war-god Skanda.

The earliest text titled Skanda Purana likely existed by the 8th century CE, but the Skanda Purana that has survived into the modern era exists in many versions. It is considered as a living text, which has been widely edited, over many centuries, creating numerous variants. The common elements in the variant editions encyclopedically cover cosmogony, mythology, genealogy, dharma, festivals, gemology, temples, geography, discussion of virtues and evil, of theology and of the nature and qualities of Shiva as the Absolute and the source of true knowledge.

The editions of Skanda purana text also provide an encyclopedic travel handbook with meticulous Tirtha

Mahatmya (pilgrimage tourist guides), containing geographical locations of pilgrimage centres in India, Nepal and Tibet, with related legends, parables, hymns and stories.

This Mahāpurāṇa, like others, is attributed to the sage Vyasa.

5.2 Date of Composition of Skanda Purana

The manuscript is believed to be dated around 8th century CE, on paleographic grounds. This suggests that the original text existed before this time. The oldest surviving palm-leaf manuscript of Skanda Purana to 810 CE, but earlier versions of the text likely existed in the 8th century CE. The text specifies holy places and details about the 4th and 5th-century Citraratha of Andhra Pradesh, and thus may have an earlier origin. The oldest versions of the Skanda purana texts have been discovered in the Himalayan region of South Asia such as Nepal, and the northeastern states of India such as Assam. The critical editions of the text, for scholarly studies, rely on the Nepalese manuscripts.

Additional texts style themselves as khandas (sections) of Skanda purana, but these came into existence after the 12th century. It is unclear if their root texts did belong to the Skanda purana, and in some cases replaced the corresponding chapters of the original. The version of the earliest known recension was later expanded in two later versions namely the

Revakhanda and Ambikakhanda recensions. The only surviving manuscript of the Revakhanda recension is from 1682 C.E.. The four surviving manuscripts of the Ambikakhhnda recension are of a later period and contains much more alterations.

There are a number of texts and manuscripts that bear the title Skanda Purana. Some of these texts, except for the title, have little in common with the well-known Skanda purana traced to the 1st millennium CE. The original text has accrued several additions, resulting in several different versions. It is, therefore, very difficult to establish an exact date of composition for the Skanda Purana.

5.3 Structure of Skanda Purana

Stylistically, the Skanda Purana is related to the Mahabharata, and it appears that its composers borrowed from the Mahabharata. The two texts employ similar stock phrases and compounds that are not found in the Ramayana. Some of the mythology mentioned in the present version of the Skanda Purana is undoubtedly post-Gupta period, consistent with that of medieval South India. This indicates that several additions were made to the original text over the centuries. The Kashi Khanda, for example, acquired its present form around the mid-13th century CE. The latest part of the text might have been composed in as late as the 15th century CE.[22]

5.4 Contents of Skanda Purana

5.4.1 Tirtha: the Holy Pilgrimage

Tirtha are of three kinds:

(i) Jangam Tirtha is to a place movable, of a sadhu, a rishi, a guru,

(ii) Sthawar Tirtha is to a place immovable, like Benaras, Hardwar, Mount Kailash, holy rivers, and

(iii) Manas Tirtha is to a place of mind, of truth, charity, patience, compassion, soft speech, soul.

—Skanda Purana

The whole corpus of texts which are considered as part of the Skanda Purana is grouped in two ways. According to one tradition, these are grouped in six saṁhitās, each of which consists of several khaṇḍas. According to another tradition, these are grouped in seven khaṇḍas, each named after a major pilgrimage region or site. The chapters are Mahatmyas, or travel guides for pilgrimage tourists.

5.4.2 The seven khandas

The Maheśvara Khaṇḍa consists of 3 sections:

(i) the Kedāra Khaṇḍa (35 chapters, Kedarnath Tirtha region, north India)

(ii) the Kaumārikā Khaṇḍa or Kumārikā Khaṇḍa (66 chapters, Mahisagara-samgama-tirtha or Cambay pilgrimage region, west India), and

(iii) the Arunācala Khaṇḍa or Arunācala Māhātmya (37 chapters, Tiruvannamalai Tirtha region, south India), further divided into two parts:

1. Pūrvārdha (13 chapters), and

2. Uttarārdha (24 chapters)

The Viṣṇu Khaṇḍa or Vaiṣṇava Khaṇḍa consists of nine sections:

(i) Veṅkaṭācalamāhātmya (40 chapters, Tirupati Tirtha region, south India),

(ii) Puruṣottamakṣetramāhātmya (49 chapters, Puri Odisha Tirtha region, east India),

(iii) Badarikāśramamāhātmya (8 chapters, Badrinath Tirtha region, north India),

(iv) Kārttikamāsamāhātmya (36 chapters),

(v) Mārgaśirṣamāsamāhātmya 17 chapters, Mathura Tirtha region),

(vi) Bhāgavatamāhātmya (4 chapters),

(vii) Vaiśākhamāsamāhātmya (25 chapters),

(viii) Ayodhyāmāhātmya (10 chapters, Ayodhya Tirtha region), and

(ix) Vāsudevamāhātmya (32 chapters).

The Brahma Khaṇḍa has three sections (four in some manuscripts):

(i) Setumāhātmya (52 chapters, Rama Setu Tirtha region, Tamil Nadu and towards Sri Lanka),

(ii) Dharmāraṇya Khaṇḍa (40 chapters), and

(iii) Uttara Khaṇḍa or Brahmottara Khaṇḍa (22 chapters).

The Kāśī Khaṇḍa (100 chapters, Varanasi and Vindya Tirtha region) is divided into two parts:

(i) Pūrvārdha (50 chapters), and

(ii) Uttarārdha (50 chapters).

The Āvantya Khaṇḍa consists of:

(i) Avantikṣetramāhātmya (71 chapters, Ujjain Tirtha region),

(ii) Caturaśītiliṅgamāhātmya (84 chapters), and

(iii) Revā Khaṇḍa (Thought to have 232 chapters.

The manuscripts attest this is actually the original Reva Khanda of Vayu Purana which was wrongly included in the Skanda Purana by Veṅkateśvara Steam Press in 1910 and all publications of the Skanda after it. The one belonging to the Skanda has 116 chapters.

The Nāgara Khaṇḍa (279 chapters) consists of Tirtha-māhātmya.

The Prabhāsa Khaṇḍa (491 chapters) consists of four sections:

(i) Prabhāsakṣetramāhātmya (365 chapters, Saurashtra and Somanatha Tirtha region, west India),

(ii) Vastrāpathakṣetramāhātmya (19 chapters, Girnar Tirtha region),

(iii) Arvuda Khaṇḍa (63 chapters, Aravalli Range Rajasthan Tirtha region), and

(iv) Dvārakāmāhātmya (44 chapters, Dwarka Gujarat Tirtha region).

5.4.3 The six samhitas

The second type of division of the Skanda Purana is found in some texts like Hālasyamāhātmya of the Agastya Saṁhitā or the Śaṁkarī Saṁhitā, Sambhava Kaṇḍa of the Śaṁkarī Saṁhitā, Śivamāhātmya Khaṇḍa of the Sūta Saṁhitā and Kālikā Khaṇḍa of the Sanatkumāra Saṁhitā. According to these texts, the Skanda Purana consists of six saṁhitās (sections):

— the Sanatkumāra Saṁhitā,

— the Sūta Saṁhitā,

— the Śaṁkarī Saṁhitā,

— the Vaiṣṇavī Saṁhitā,

— the Brāhmī Saṁhitā, and

— the Saura Saṁhitā.

The manuscripts of the Sanatkumāra Saṁhitā, the Śaṁkarī Saṁhitā, the Sūta Saṁhitā and the Saura Saṁhitā are extant. A manuscript of a commentary on the Sūta Saṁhitā by Madhavācārya is also available. These texts discuss cosmogony, theology, philosophical questions on virtues and vice, questions such as what is evil, the origin of evil, how to deal with and cure evil.

5.4.4 The other texts

The manuscripts of several other texts which claim to be part of the Skanda Purāṇa are found partially or wholly. Some of the notable regional texts amongst these are: Himavat Khaṇḍa which contains Nepalamahatmya (30 chapters, Nepal Tirtha region), Kanakādri Khaṇḍa, Bhīma Khaṇḍa, Śivarahasya Khaṇḍa, Sahyādri Khaṇḍa, Ayodhyā Khaṇḍa, Mathurā Khaṇḍa and Pātāla Khaṇḍa.

Kaverimahatmya presents stories and a pilgrim guide for the Kaveri river (Karnataka) and Coorg Tirtha region. Vivsamitrimahatmya presents mythology and a guide for the Vadodara Tirtha region.

The oldest known 1st-millennium palm-leaf manuscripts of this text mention many major Hindu pilgrimage sites, but do not describe Kailash-Manasarovar. The later versions do, particularly in Manasakhanda.

5.5 The narratives in Skanda Purana

The Skanda Purana, like many Puranas, include the legends of the Daksha's sacrifice, Shiva's sorrow, churning of the ocean (Samudra manthan) and the emergence of Amrita, the story of the demon Tarakasura, the birth of Goddess Parvati, her pursuit of Shiva, and her marriage to Lord Shiva, among others.

The central aim of the Skanda purana text, is to sanctify the geography and landscape of South Asia, and legitimize the regional Shaiva communities across the land, as it existed at the time the edition was produced. The text reflects the political uncertainties, the competition with Vaishnavism, and the cultural developments with the Pashupata Hindus during the periods it was composed.

5.6 Skanda Purana Manuscripts

The Skanda Purana manuscripts have been found in Nepal, Tamil Nadu and other parts of India. The Skanda Purana is among of the oldest dated manuscripts discovered in Nepal. A palm-leaf manuscript of the text is preserved at the National Archives of Nepal (NAK 2–229), and its digital version has been archived by Nepal-German Manuscript Preservation Project. It is likely that the manuscript was copied by the scribe on March 10 811 CE, though there is some uncertainty with this date because the samvat of this manuscript is unclear. This manuscript was discovered as one in a group of seven different texts bound together. The group included fourteen manuscripts mostly Buddhist, six of which are very old Saddharma Pundarika Sutra manuscripts, one of Upalisutra, one Chinese Buddhist text, and one Bhattikavya Buddhist yamaka text. The Skanda Purana found in this manuscripts collection is written in transitional Gupta script, Sanskrit.

The 1910 edition included seven khaṇḍas (parts): Maheśvara, Viṣṇu or Vaiṣṇava, Brahma, Kāśī, Āvantya, Nāgara and Prabhāsa. In 1999–2003, an English translation of this text was published.

5.7 Why Is Ganesha the Lord Of Obstacles? - Story in Skanda Purana

An interesting story in the Skanda Purana mentions why Ganesha is the Lord of Obstacles? One who removes obstacles and one who creates obstacles. It is said that all kinds of people attained moksha as a result of visiting the Someshwara Temple (Somnath temple in Gujarat) – due to a boon granted by Shiva to Soma (moon god). People stopped all sort of ascetic practices, austerities and sacrifices. All sinners were purified by visiting Somnath. This caused imbalance in the universe.

Indra, the king of Devas, wanted to find a solution to the problem and approached Shiva. He said He could not change the boon given to Soma. Shiva directed Indra to Goddess Parvati.

Goddess Parvati gauged the situation and Mother Goddess decided to rectify the imbalance.

She slowly rubbed Her body and from Her body appeared a four-armed divine being with an elephant head. This was Ganesha.

Ganesha was asked to create obstacles in the path of sinners who visited Somnath Temple to attain Moksha. Ganesha thus created impediments in the path of sinners and all people who performed Adharma. They were caught in the web of desire and possessions. They danced to the tune of the senses. Thus he created obstacles in the path of Adharmic people.

Goddess Parvati also asked Ganesha to remove the obstacles from path of all those who followed Dharma. To those who follow Dharma, he is the remover of all obstacles. He helps them attain moksha.

Thus Ganesha became the Lord of Obstacles.

Vighna Naashaka: Various Puranas assert that Ganesha Puja bestows vighna nivaarana, Roga Mukti by Surya Puja, Atma shuddhi by Agni puja, Moksha Laabha by Vishna puja, Jnaana prapti by Shiva puja and Ishvarya-Sukha- Laabha by Durga puja. Varaha Purana clarified that in the days of yore, there was often the tendency of Satyavartis or persons of virtue were invariably subjected to difficulties while others of negativity and evil were scot free. While realizing the tendency, Lord Shiva created akaasha like Figure named Ganesha to reverse and reform the tendency of evil to be destroyed and save the persons of virtue as the slogan of 'Satyameva Jayate'. Skanda Purana refers to Ganesha Puja ab initio of 'Samudra Madhana' or the Great Churning of Ksheera Sagara madhana by both Devas and Danavas and thus the end result was 'Amrita', despite massive difficulties like steadying of Mandhara Mountain causing Kurmaavatara of Vishnu and haalaahala agni contained by Shiva as Garala kantha! Linga Purana asserted that Shiva emphasized the absolute necessity of initiating any task of Shrouta- Smaarta-Loukika karmas. The Purana exclaims that while Tri Murtis and all the Deva Devis make it a fixed necessity for initiating any task, could humans, be they are high intellectuals or below normal, be exceptions unless they are blessed by Ganesha!

Skanda Purana assures:

Yo kaamamabhidhyaaya Gana naadham prapujayet,

sa tam sarvamaapnoti 10 Maheshvara vacho yathaa/

Maheshwara directed all those seeking fulfillment of desires ought to venerate foremost. Ganesha Purana is emphatic that Ganesha's agrapujyata is 'anivarya' or a firmly established truism- be it for any kind of deed- be it vidyaarambha-griha pravesha-yaatraa rambha-shtouta-smaartadhaarmika-loukika karyaas; failure to do so by way of Ganesha Smarana-Vandana-Pujana is asking for troubles as history is replete with numberless instances as proven in Purana- Itihaasaas.

Abheeshta Siddhi: Skanda Purana assures:

Aputro labhate putram dhana heeno mahaddhanam

shatrujjyati sangraame smritvaa tam Gana naayakam/

Mere thoughtful greeting to Ganesha with sincerity would fulfill the desire for excellent progeny, prosperity and victory in battles and encounters as well as success in life. The Skanda Purana in varied references states:

Yo naaree patinaa tyaktaa durbhagaa cha virupitaa,
saasoubhaagyavaapnoti Gananaadhasya pujayaa/

Sarvakaaryeshu ye martyaah purvamenam Ganaadhipam,
smarishyanti na vai teshaam kaaryahaanirbhavishyati/

Ye tvaam sampujayishyanti karyaarambheshu sarvatah,
kaarya siddhinam sandeshasteshaam bhruuyaad
giraa mama/

Vivaahe kalahe yuddhe prasthaane krishi karmaani,
praveshecha smared yastu bhaktipuurvam Vinaayakam/

Tasya yad vaancchitam sarvam prasaadaat tasya siddhiti/

Those women deserted by their husbands due to their physical or mental disabilities are surely rid of their misfortunes by their dedicated Ganesha Puja. What all tasks are initiated by Ganesha Puja are sure to be succeeded without any hurdle or negativity. Be it in the context of weddings, or wars, or any kind of field works like agriculture and so on, Ganesha Puja with sincerity ought to reap success undoubtedly.

Skanda Purana is quoted further:

Praataruddhhaya yo matryah smeded Devam Vinaayakam,

tasya taddinajaataani siddhim krityaani yaantih/

Smritvaa vaa pujayitvaa vaa yah kaaryaani karishyati,

bhavishyant na sandehaasosyaa vichalichaani cha/

Parama Shiva assures that human beings who initiate their tasks and duties even as they conclude their night long sleep and wake up remember Ganesha with their sincere prayers to Him ought to proceed with self-confidence , undoubted and smooth success throughout the day till their bed time.

CHAPTER 6

LORD GANESHA IN SHIVA PURANA

6.1 Introduction to Shiva Purana

The Shiva Purana is one of eighteen major texts of the Purana genre of Tamil texts in Hinduism, and part of the Shaivism literature corpus. It primarily revolves around the Hindu God Shiva and Goddess Parvati, but references and reveres all gods.

The Shiva Purana asserts that it once consisted of 100,000 verses set out in twelve Samhitas (Books), however the Purana adds that it was abridged by Sage Vyasa before being taught to Romaharshana. The surviving manuscripts exist in many different versions and content, with one major version with seven books (traced to South India), another with six books, while the third version traced to the medieval Bengal region of the Indian Subcontinent with no books but two large sections called Purva-Khanda (Previous Section) and Uttara-Khanda (Later Section). The two versions that include books, title some of the books same and others differently. The Shiva Purana, like other Puranas in Hindu literature, was likely a living text, which was routinely edited, recast and revised over a long period of time. The oldest manuscript of surviving texts was likely composed around 10th- to

162

11th-century CE. Some chapters of currently surviving Shiva Purana manuscripts were likely composed after the 14th-century.

The Shiva Purana contains chapters with Shiva-centred cosmology, mythology, relationship between Gods, ethics, yoga, tirtha (pilgrimage) sites, bhakti, rivers and geography, and other topics. The text is an important source of historic information on different types and theology behind Shaivism in early 2nd-millennium CE. The oldest surviving chapters of the Shiva Purana have significant Advaita Vedanta philosophy, which is mixed in with theistic elements of bhakti.

In the 19th and 20th century, the Vayu Purana was sometimes titled as Shiva Purana, and sometimes proposed as a part of the complete Shiva Purana. With the discovery of more manuscripts, modern scholarship considers the two texts as different, with Vayu Purana as the more older text composed sometime before the 2nd-century CE. Some scholars list it as a Mahapurana, while some state it is an Upa purana.

6.2 Date of Shiva Purana

The date and authors of Shiva Purana are unknown. No authentic data is available. Scholars estimate that the oldest chapters in the surviving manuscript were likely composed around the 10- to 11th-centuries CE, which has not stood the test of carbon dating technology hence on that part we must rely on the text itself which tells when it was composed. Certain books and chapters in currently surviving Shiva Purana manuscripts were likely composed later, some after the 14th-century. The Shiva Purana, like other Puranas in Hindu literature, were routinely edited, recast and revised over the centuries.

The Bombay manuscript published in the 19th-century is rarer, and likely the older than other versions published from eastern and southern India.

6.3 Contents of Shiva Purana

The Vidyeshvara Samhita, also called Vighneśa Samhita or Vidyalaya Samhita, appears in both editions, is free of mythology found in some other samhitas, and is dedicated to describing the greatness and the bhakti of Shiva, particularly through the icon of Linga. This section is also notable for mentioning both Shaiva Agamas and Tantric texts, but frequently quoting from the Vedas and asserting that the text is the essence of the Vedic teaching and the Vedanta. The chapters of this shared samhita in different versions of the Shiva Purana includes a description of India's geography and rivers from north and south India so often it is difficult to gauge if this part was composed in north or south India.

The Jnana samhita in one manuscript shares content with Rudra samhita of the other manuscript, presents cosmology and mythology, and is notable for its discussion of saguna andnirguna Shiva.

The text discusses goddesses and gods, dedicates parts of chapters praising Vishnu and Brahma, as well as those related to avatars such as Krishna. It asserts that one must begin with karma-yajna, thereon step by step with tapo-yajna, then self-study, then regular meditation, ultimately to jnana-yajna and yoga to achieve sayujya (intimate union) with Shiva within. The text emphasizes bhakti and yoga, rather than bookish learning of the Vedas.

The Shiva Purana dedicates chapters to Shaiva-Advaita philosophy, like Linga Purana and other Shaivism-related Puranas, advocating it as a system for Salvation. The text also presents the Brahman as satchidananda theme, with masculine and feminine Shiva-Shakti as a unity, and perception of plurality-discrimination as a form of nescience. Love-Driven Devotionalism (Bhakti), asserts the text, leads to knowledge, and such love combined with knowledge leads to attracting saintly people and Guru, and with them one attains Liberation, states Shiva Purana. These ideas are similar to those found in Devi-related Puranas and Shakti Literature.

6.4 Birth of Ganesha (Chapter 13, Shiva Purana)

Shiva Purana mentions that in in the Shveta Varaha Kalpa Devi Parvati mentioned to her maids Jaya and Vijaya that there was none else worthy of worship excepting her own body sweat which eventually took the form of an outstanding form of a boy named Ganesha. The Purana further states: When Nandi was asked to bar entry into the Interior Place of Parvati as She was taking bath, Nandi no doubt prevented but Lord Shiva still entered and She was not amused. She decided to create an idol of a boy which was infused with life and empowered Him to challenge anybody with the necessary powers. The boy followed the instruction and did not allow entry even to Shiva. The Pramadha ganas were asked to teach a lesson to the boy by Shiva but they were defeated in no time. Shiva Himself decided to force His entry but to no avail. Finally, an irritated Shiva snapped the boy's head and Parvati became furious and Her angry manifestations surprised Shiva Himself. She insisted that the boy be brought to life forth with. Shiva suggested locating anybody sleeping in the northern direction and the Shivaganas were able to trace only an elephant. The severed head of the boy was fixed with that of the elephant and He was revived. The assembly of Deities who first fought with the boy and witnessed the entire scene earlier decided that any function in the World ought to be commenced with worship of Ganesha foremost as He is the Lord of preventing impediments and of providing success. Ganesha's worship on Bhadrapada Sukla Chathurdhi is a must all over Bharata desha as one is dreaded of becoming a victim of undeserving blames since Moon

God received a curse from Ganesha that whoever saw the Moon on the particular Chaturdhi night without worshipping Him would become a sure target!

According to Chapter 13 of Shiva Purana:

Sūta said:

1. On hearing the marvelously excellent story of the slayer of Tāraka thus, Nārada was highly delighted and he lovingly asked Brahmā.

2. O lord of gods and people, O storehouse of Shiva's cult, the excellent story of Kārttikeya, far better than nectar, has been heard by me.

3. Now I wish to hear the excellent story of Ganesha, the details of his divine nativity, auspicious of the auspicious.

4. On hearing the words of Nārada the great sage, Brahmā became delighted and replied to him remembering Shiva.

Brahmā said:

5. Due to the difference of Kalpas, the story of the birth of Ganesha is told in different ways. According to one account he is born of the great lord. His head looked at by Shani was cut off and an elephant's head was put on him.

6. Now we narrate the story of the birth of Ganesha in Śvetakalpa when his head was cut off by the merciful Shiva.

7. No suspicion need be entertained, O sage. Shiva is certainly the cause of enjoyment and protection. He is the lord of all. Shiva is possessed as well as devoid of attributes.

8. It is by His divine sport that the entire universe is created, sustained and annihilated. O excellent sage, listen to what is relevant to the context, with attention.

9. A long time had lapsed after the marriage of Shiva and His return to Kailasha that Ganesha was born.

10. Once the friends Jāyā and Vijaya conferred with Parvati and discussed.

11. All the Ganas of Rudra carry out the orders of Shiva. They all, Nandin, Bhṇṇgin and others are in a way our own.

12. Pramathas are numerous. But none of them can be called our own. They all stand at the portals, subservient to Shiva's behests.

13. They also may be called our own but our mind is not in unison with them. Hence, O sinless lady, one, our own must be created.

Brahmā said:

14. Goddess Parvati to whom this charming suggestion was made by the two friends considered it wholesome and resolved to carry it out.

15. Once when Parvati was taking her bath, Sadasiva rebuked Nandin and came into the inner apartment.

16. The mother of the universe, seeing the untimely arrival of Shiva in the midst of her bath and

toilet stood up. The beautiful lady was very shy then.

17. The goddess decided that her friend's suggestion would be conducive to her good and was so enthusiastic.

18. At the time when the incident occurred, Parvati, the great Māyā, the great goddess, thought as follows.

19. "There must be a servant of my own who will be expert in his duties. He must not stray from my behest even a speck."

20. Thinking thus the goddess created a person with all the characteristics, out of the dirt from her body.

21. He was spotless and handsome in every part of his body. He was huge in size and had all brilliance, strength and valor.

22-23. She gave him various clothes and ornaments. She blessed him with benediction and said—"You are my son. You are my own. I have none else to call my own". Thus addressed the person bowed to her and said:

Ganesha said:

24. "What is your order? I shall accomplish what you command." Thus addressed, Parvati replied to her son.

Parvati said:

25. "O dear, listen to my words. Work as my gatekeeper from today. You are my son. You are my own. It is not otherwise. There is none-else who belongs to me.

26. O good son, without my permission, no one, by any means, shall intrude my apartment. I tell you the fact."

Brahmā said:

27. O sage, saying this, she gave him a hard stick. On seeing his handsome features she was delighted.

28. Out of love and mercy she embraced and kissed him. She placed him armed with a staff at her entrance as the gatekeeper.

29. Then the son of the goddess, of great heroic power, stayed at the doorway armed with a staff with a desire to do what was good to her.

30. Thus placing her son at the doorway, Parvati began to take bath with her friends, unworried.

31. O excellent sage, at this very moment Shiva who is eagerly indulgent and an expert in various divine sports came near the door.

32. Not knowing that he was lord Shiva, the consort of Parvati, Gaṇeśa said—"O sir, without my mother's permission you shall not go in now".

33. My mother has entered the bath. Where are you going now? Go away" saying thus, he took up his staff to ward him off.

34. On seeing him Shiva said "O foolish fellow, whom are you forbidding? O wicked knave, don't you know me? I Shiva, none else".

35. Thereupon Ganesha beat Shiva with the staff. Shiva, expert in various sports, became infuriated and spoke to his son thus.

Shiva said:

36. "You are a fool, You do not know that I am Shiva, the husband of Parvati. O boy, I go in my own house. Why do you forbid me?"

Brahmā said:

37. When lord Shiva tried to enter the house, Ganesha became infuriated, O brahmin, and struck him with his staff once again.

38. Then Shiva too became furious. He commanded his own Ganas—"Who is this fellow here? What is he doing? O Ganas, enquire."

39. After saying this, the furious Shiva stood outside the house. The lord, following the worldly conventions, is capable of various wonderful sports.

6.5 Ganesha's Argument and Wrangle (Chapter 14, Shiva Purana)

Brahmā said:

1. The infuriated Ganas of Shiva at his bidding went there and questioned the son of Parvati who stood at the gate.

Shiva's Ganas said:

2. "Who are you? Whence do you come? What do you propose to do? If you have a desire to remain alive go away from here."

Brahmā said:

3. On hearing their words, the son of Parvati who was armed with the staff spoke to the Ganas as follows.

Ganesha said:

4. O "handsome fellows, who are you? Whence have you come? Go away. Why have you come here and why do you stand in opposition to me?"

Brahmā said:

5. On hearing his words, Shiva's Ganas of great heroism and arrogance laughingly spoke to one another.

6. After conferring with one another, the infuriated Parada's of Śiva replied to Gaṇeśa, the doorkeeper.

Śiva's Ganas said:

7. "Listen. We are the excellent Ganas of Shiva. We are his doorkeepers. We have come here to throw you out at the bidding of lord Shiva.

8. Considering you too, as one of the Ganas, we are not going to kill you. Otherwise you would have been killed. Better stay away yourself. Why do you court death?"

Brahmā said:

9. Though warned thus, Ganesha, the son of Parvati, stood fearless. He did not leave his post at the door. He rebuked Śiva's Ganas.

10. After hearing his words, the Ganas of Śiva went back and informed Śiva about his stand.

11. O sage, on hearing their words, lord Shiva of wonderful divine sports, following the worldly conventions rebuked his Ganas.

Lord Shiva said:

12. "Who is this fellow? What does he say? He is standing there haughtily as though he is our enemy. What will that wicked knave do? Certainly he wants to die.

13. Why? Are you dastardly eunuchs to stand here helplessly and complain to me about him. Let this new doorkeeper be thrown out."

Brahmā said:

14. Thus commanded by lord Shiva of wonderful sports the Ganas returned to the place and spoke to the doorkeeper.

Shiva's Ganas said:

15. O gatekeeper, who are you standing here? Why have you been stationed here? Why don't you care for us. How can you thus remain alive?

16. We are here the duly appointed doorkeepers. What are you saying? A jackal sitting on a lion's seat wishes for happiness.

17. O fool, you will roar only as long as you do not feel the brunt of our attack. Erelong you will fall by feeling the same."

18. Thus taunted by them, Ganesha became furious and took the staff with his hands and struck the Ganas even as they continued to speak harsh words.

19. Then the fearless Ganesha, son of Parvati rebuked the heroic Ganas of Shiva and spoke as follows.

The son of Parvati said:

20. "Get away. Get away. Or I shall give you a foretaste of my fierce valor. You will be the laughing-stock of all."

21. On hearing these words of Ganesha, the Ganas of Śiva spoke to one another.

Shiva's Ganas said:

22. What shall be done? Where shall we go? Why shall we not act? Bounds of decency are observed by us. He would not have acted thus, otherwise.

Brahmā said:

23. Then the Ganas of Shiva went to Shiva who was standing at the distance of a Krośa from Kailasha and spoke to him.

24. Shiva ridiculed them all. The trident-armed great lord of fierce temperament spoke to his Ganas who professed to be heroes.

Shiva said:

25. "Hello, Ganas, impotent wretches, you profess to be heroic but are never so. You are unfit to stand before me and speak. If he is only taunted he will speak in similar tone again.

26. Go and beat him. Someone among you may be competent to do so. Why should I speak more? He must be driven away."

Brahmā said:

27. O great sage, when rebuked thus by lord Shiva, the excellent Ganas went back and spoke to him.

Shiva's Ganas said:

28. Hello you boy there, listen. Why do you speak so arrogantly? You go away from here. If not, your death is certain.

Brahmā said:

29. On hearing the words of Shiva's servants the son of Parvati became unhappy and thought "What shall I do?"

30. In the meantime, the goddess heard the noise of this wrangle between the Ganas and the doorkeeper, then looked at her friend and spoke. "Go and see."

31. The friend came to the door and saw them for a moment. She understood the whole matter. She was delighted and returned to Parvati.

32. O sage, coming back she reported the matter to Parvati as it had occurred.

The friend said:

33. O great Goddess, the heroic Ganas of Shiva arc taunting and rebuking our own Gaṇa who is standing at the door.

34. How do these Ganas and Shiva enter your apartment suddenly without looking to your convenience? This is not good for you.

35. Even after undergoing the misery of rebuke etc. he, our Gaṇa, has done well in not allowing anyone in.

36. What is more? They are arguing too. When the argument has started, they cannot come in happily.

37. Now that they have started the argument let them conquer him and enter victoriously. Not otherwise, my dear friend.

38. When this man belonging to us is taunted, it amounts to our being taunted. Hence, O gentle lady, you shall not abandon your prestige of high order.

39. Shiva always squeezes you like a crab, O Satī. What will he do now? His pride will take a favorable turn for us.

Brahmā said:

40. Alas, being subservient to Shiva's wish, Parvati stood there for a moment.

41. Then taking up a haughty mood she spoke to herself.

Parvati said:

42. "Alas, he did not wait for a moment. Why should he force his way in? What shall be done now? Or shall I adopt a humble attitude.

43. What is to happen happens. What is done cannot be altered?" After saying this, Parvati sent her again lovingly.

44. The friend came to the door and told Gaṇeśa what Parvati had said with affection.

The friend said:

45. O gentle sir, well done. Let them not enter forcibly. What are these Ganas before you? Can they win a person like you?

46. Whether good or bad let your duty be done. If you are conquered there will be no further enmity at all.

Brahmā said:

47. On hearing the words of the friend and his mother Gopeshvara became highly delighted, strengthened and lifted up.

48. Girting up his loins, tying his turban firmly and clapping his calves and thighs, he spoke fearlessly to all the Ganas.

Ganesha said:

49. I am the son of Parvati. You are the Ganas of Shiva. Both of us are thus equal. Let your duty be done, now.

50. You are all doorkeepers. How is it that I am not? You are standing there and I am standing here. This is certain.

51. When it is certain that you are standing here, you must carry out the directions of Shiva.

52. O heroes, now I have to carry out the orders of Parvati faithfully. I have decided what is proper.

53. Hence, O Ganas of Shiva, you shall listen with attention. You shall not enter the apartment either forcibly or humbly.

Brahmā said:

54. The Ganas when decisively told by Ganesha became ashamed. They went to Shiva. After bowing to him they stood in front of him.

55. Then they acquainted him with that news of wonderful nature. They joined their palms, stooped their shoulders, eulogized Shiva and stood in front of him.

56. On hearing the detailed news mentioned by his Ganas, Shiva replied following the worldly conventions.

Shiva said:

57. O Ganas, hear you all. A battle may not be a proper course. You are all my own. He is Parvati's Gaṇa.

58. But if we are going to be humble, there is likely to be a rumor: "Shiva is subservient to his wife." O Ganas, this is certainly derogatory to me.

59. The policy of meeting an action with another (Tit for tat) is a weighty one. That single-handed Gaṇa is a mere boy. What valor can be expected of him?

60. O Ganas, you are all experts in warfare and reputed to be so in the world. You are my own

men. How can you forsake war and demean yourselves?

61. How can a woman be obdurate especially with her husband? Parvati will certainly derive the fruit of what she has done.

62. Hence, my heroic men, listen to my words with attention. This war has to be fought by all means. Let what is in store happen."

Brahmā said:

63. O excellent sage, O brahmin, after saying thus, Shiva an adept in various divine sports became silent observing the ways of the world.

6.6 Ganesha's Battle (Chapter 15, Shiva Purana)

Brahmā said:

1. When Śiva told them thus, they came to a decisive resolution. They got ready and went to Śiva's palace.

2. On seeing the excellent Ganas, fully equipped for war, coming, Gaṇeśa spoke thus to them.

Gaṇeśa said:

3. Welcome to the leaders of Ganas, carrying out the behests of Śiva. I am only one and that too a mere boy carrying out the directions of Parvati.

4. Yet let the goddess see the strength of her son. Let Śiva see the strength of his Ganas too.

5. The fight between the parties of Parvati and Śiva is the one between a strong army and a boy. You are all experts in warfare and have fought in many a battle.

6. I have never fought in a battle before. I am a mere boy. I am going to fight now. Still if you are put to shame, it will be shameful to Śiva and Parvati.

7. But that will not happen to me. If I am put to shame, the contrary will happen to me. Parvati and Śiva will be put to shame but not I.

8. O leader of the Ganas, the war shall be fought after realising this. You shall look up to your lord and I to my mother.

9. What sort of a fight shall be fought? Let what is destined to occur, occur. No one in the three worlds can ward it off.

Brahmā said:

10. When thus taunted and rebuked they rushed towards him with big batons, decorating their arms and taking up different kinds of weapons.

11. Gnashing their teeth, grunting and bellowing and calling out "See, See", the Ganas rushed at him.

12. Nandin came first and caught hold of his leg. He pulled at it. Bhṇṇgin then rushed at him and caught hold of his other leg.

13. Before the Ganas of Śiva had time to pull his legs Gaṇeśa struck a blow at their hands and got his legs free.

14. Then seizing a big iron club and standing at the doorway he smashed the ganas.

15. Some got their hands broken, others got their backs smothered. The heads of others were shattered and the foreheads of some were crushed.

16. The knees of some were fractured, the shoulders of others were blasted. Those who came in front were hit in the chest.

17. Some fell on the ground, some fled in various directions, some got their legs broken and some fled to Śiva.

18-19. Now none among them stood face to face. Just as deer flee to any direction on seeing a lion, the Ganas, who were thousands in number fled in that manner. Then Gaṇeśa returned to doorway and stood there.

20. He was seen as the annihilator of all in the manner of Yama, the terrible god of death at the end of a Kalpa.

21. At this time, urged by Nārada, all the gods including Viṣṇu and Indra came there.

22. Standing in front of Śiva and bowing to him with a desire to secure good for him they said—"O lord, be pleased to command us.

23. You are the great Brahman, the lord of all, the creator, the sustainer and the annihilator of all created things. All are your servants.

24. You are intrinsically devoid of attributes but by means of your sports you assume Rajasekar, Sattvika and Tamasic forms. O lord, what sort of sport you are indulging in, now?"

Brahmā said:

25. O excellent sage, on hearing their words and seeing the Ganas completely shattered, lord Śiva told them everything.

26. O excellent sage, Śiva, the lord of all, the consort of Parvati, then laughingly told me, Brahmā.

Śiva said:

27. O Brahmā, listen. A boy is standing at the entrance to my house. He is very strong. He has a staff in his hand. He prevents me from entering the house.

28. He strikes very dexterously. He has destroyed many of my Parada's. He has forcefully defeated my Ganas.

29. O Brahmā, you alone should go there. This strong boy shall be propitiated. O Brahmā, you shall do everything to bring him under control.

Brahmā said:

30. On hearing the words of the lord and unable to know the reality, being deluded by ignorance, O dear, I went near Gaṇeśa accompanied by the sages.

31. On seeing me approaching, the powerful Gaṇeśa came to me very furiously and plucked my moustache and beard.

32. "Forgive me. Forgive me, O lord. I have not come for fighting. I am a brahmin and shall be blessed. I have come to make peace and I will cause no harm."

33. While I said thus, O brahmin, the heroic Gaṇeśa, the boy of great valour uncommon to the boys took up the iron club.

34. On seeing the powerful Gaṇeśa seizing the iron club I began to run away immediately.

35. The others too who were shouting "Go, Go" were struck down with the iron club. Some fell themselves and some were felled by him.

36. Some of them fled to Śiva in a trice and intimated to him the details of the incident.

37. On seeing them in that plight and on hearing the news, Śiva, an adept in sports became very angry.

38. He issued directives to Indra and other gods, to the Ganas led by the six-faced Kumara and to goblins, ghosts and spirits.

39. At the bidding of Śiva they all desired to kill Gaṇeśa. Lifting up their weapons in a suitable manner they came there from all directions.

40. Whatever weapon they had was hurled on Gaṇeśa with force.

41. There was a great hue and cry in all the three worlds consisting of the mobile and immobile. The inhabitants of the worlds were in a great fix and uncertainty.

42. "Brahma's life span is not over, but the whole universe is undergoing untimely destruction. Certainly it is due to Śiva's wish.

43. The six faced deity and the other gods who came there failed to use their weapons effectively. They were very much surprised.

44. In the meantime, goddess, the mother of the universe, of special knowledge, came to know of the entire incident and was very furious.

45. O great sage, the goddess created two Saktis then and there for the assistance of her own Gaṇa.

46. O great sage, one Śakti assumed a very fierce form and stood there opening her mouth as wide as the cavern of a dark mountain.

47. The other assumed the form of lightning. She wore many arms. She was a huge and terrible goddess ready to punish the wicked.

48. The weapons hurled by the gods and the Ganas were caught in the mouth and hurled back at them.

49. None of the weapons of the gods was seen anywhere around the iron club of Gaṇeśa. This wonderful feat was performed by them.

50. A single boy stirred and churned the vast impassable army in the same manner as great mountain[2] churned the ocean of milk formerly.

51. Indra and other gods were struck by him, singlehanded. The Ganas of Śiva became agitated and distressed then.

52. Gasping frequently for their breath, being utterly shaken by his blows they gathered together and spoke to one another.

The gods and Ganas said:

53. "What shall be done? Where should we go? The ten directions have become visible. He is whirling the iron club right and left."

Brahmā said:

54-55. In the meantime the excellent nymphs came there with flowers and sandal paste in their hands. You and other gods who were eager to witness the fight came there. O excellent sage, the excellent pathway of the firmament was entirely filled by them.

56. Seeing the battle they were much surprised. Such a battle had never been witnessed by them before.

57. The earth with all the oceans quaked. As a result of the violent battle even mountains fell down.

58. The sky whirled with the planets and the stars. Everything was agitated. The gods fled. The Ganas too did likewise.

59. The valorous six faced deity alone did not flee. The great warrior stopped everyone and stood in front.

60. But the Ganas fought in vain with the two Saktis. The weapons of the gods and the Ganas were broken and hence withdrawn by them.

61. Those that tarried went to Śiva. All the gods and Ganas fled.

62. Those who went in a body to Śiva bowed to him again and again and asked Śiva immediately "O lord who is that excellent Gaṇa?"

63. We have heard that battles used to be fought formerly. Even now many battles are being fought. But never was such a battle seen or heard.

64. O lord, let this be pondered over a little. Otherwise no victory is possible. O lord, you alone are the saviour of the universe. There is no doubt about it."

Brahmā said:

65. On hearing their words, the furious Rudra became more furious and went there along with his Ganas.

66. The entire army of the gods along with the discus bearing Viṣṇu shouted in jubilation and followed Śiva.

67. In the meantime, bowing to Śiva, the lord of the gods with palms joined in reverence, O Nārada, you spoke as follows.

Nārada said:

68. "O lord of the gods, please listen to my words. You are the all-pervading lord and expert in various sports.

69. By indulging in a great sport, the arrogance of the Ganas has been removed by you. O Śaṅkara, the impudence of the gods too has been removed by giving this (Gaṇeśa) much strength.

70. O lord Śiva, your own wonderful strength has been known to the worlds, you who independently remove the haughtiness of everyone.

71. O lord who are favourably disposed to your devotees, do not indulge in that sport. Please honour your own Ganas and the gods suitably and make them flourish.

72. O bestower of the region of Brahman, please do not treat him leisurely but kill him in your play now." O Nārada, after saying this, you vanished from the place.

6.7 The head of Ganesha is chopped off during the battle (Chapter 16, Shiva Purana)

Brahmā said:

1. O Nārada, on hearing your words, the great lord who grants benediction to his devotees became desirous of fighting with the boy.

2. He called Viṣṇu and consulted him. Then with a great army and the gods, He, the three-eyed lord, stood face to face with him.

3. After remembering the lotus-like feet of Śiva, the gods possessing great strength, kindly glanced at by Śiva and highly jubilant, fought with him.

4. Viṣṇu of great strength, valour and skill and possessing great divine weapons and Siva's form fought with him.

5. Gaṇeśa hit all the chief gods with his staff. He hit Viṣṇu too, all of a sudden. The hero had been conferred great strength by the Saktis.

6. O sage, all the gods including Viṣṇu were hit by him with the stick. They were turned back with their strength sapped.

7. O sage, after fighting for a long time along with the army and seeing him terrific, even Śiva was greatly surprised.

8. Thinking within himself "He has to be killed only by deception and not otherwise" he stayed in the midst of the army.

9-10. When lord Śiva who though devoid of attributes had assumed the attributive form was seen in the battle, when Viṣṇu too had come thither, the gods and Ganas of Śiva were highly delighted. They joined together and became jubilant.

11. Then Gaṇeśa the heroic son of Śakti following the course of heroes, at first worshipped (i.e. struck) Viṣṇu with his staff, Viṣṇu who confers happiness to all.

12-13. "I shall cause him delusion. Then let him be killed by you, O lord. Without deception he cannot be killed. He is of Tāmasika nature and inaccessible." Thinking thus and consulting Śiva, Viṣṇu secured Śiva's permission and was engaged in the activities of delusion.

14. O sage, on seeing Viṣṇu in that manner, the two Saktis handed over their power to Gaṇeśa and became submerged.

15. When the two Saktis became submerged, Gaṇeśa with more strength infused in him hurled the iron club in the place where Viṣṇu stood.

16. Viṣṇu strenuously dodged the same after remembering Śiva, the great lord, favourably disposed towards His devotees.

17. Seeing his face on a side, the infuriated Śiva took up his trident with a desire to fight and came there.

18. Parvati's son of great strength and heroism, saw Śiva arrived there with desire to fight him to a finish, the great lord with the trident in his hand.

19. Gaṇeśa, the great hero, who had been rendered more powerful by Parvati and the Saktis remembered the lotus-like feet of his mother and struck him in his hand with his Śakti.

20. Thereupon the trident fell from the hand of Śiva of supreme soul. Seeing this, Śiva the source of great enjoyment and protection took up his bow Pināka.

21. Gaṇeśa felled that to the ground by means of his iron club. Five of his hands too were struck. He took up the trident with the other five hands.

22. "Alas, this has been more distressing even to me. What may not happen to the Ganas? Śiva who followed the worldly conventions cried out like this.

23. In the meantime the heroic Gaṇeśa endowed with the surplus power bestowed by the Saktis struck the gods and the Ganas with his iron club.

24. The gods and the Ganas smothered by that wonderful striker with the iron club went away to the ten directions. None of them remained in the battlefield.

25-27. On seeing Gaṇeśa, Viṣṇu said—"He is blessed. He is a great hero of great strength. He is valorous and fond of battle. Many gods, Danara's, Daithya's, Yakṣas, Gandharvas, and Rakṣasas I have seen. In the entire extent of the three worlds, none of them can equal Gaṇeśa in regard to brilliance, form, features, valour and other qualities."

28. Gaṇeśa, son of the Saktis whirled the iron club and hurled it at Viṣṇu even as he was saying so.

29. After remembering the lotus-like feet of Śiva, Viṣṇu took up his discus and split the iron club by means of discus.

30. Gaṇeśa hurled the piece of iron club at Viṣṇu which was caught by the bird Garuḍa and rendered futile.

31. Thus for a long time the two heroes Viṣṇu and Gaṇeśa fought with each other.

32. Again the foremost among heroes, the son of Parvati took up his staff of unrivalled power remembering Śiva and struck Viṣṇu with it.

33. Struck with that unbearable blow he fell on the ground. But he got up, quickly and fought with Parvati's son.

34. Securing this opportunity, the Trident-bearing deity came there and cut off his head with his trident.

35. O Nārada, when the head of Gaṇeśa was cut off, the armies of the gods and the Ganas stood still.

36. You, Nārada, then came and acquainted Parvati with the matter—"O proud woman, listen. You shall not cast off your pride and prestige."

37. O Nārada, saying this, you, fond of quarrels, vanished from there. You are the unchanging sage and a follower of the inclinations of Śiva.

6.8 The Resuscitation of Ganesha (Chapter 17, Shiva Purana)

Nārada said:

1. O Brahmā, of great intellect, please narrate. When the entire news was heard what did the great goddess Parvati do? I wish to hear all in fact.

Brahmā said:

2. O foremost among sages, listen. I shall mention the story of the mother of the universe in the manner that it happened afterwards.

3. When Gaṇeśa was killed, the Ganas were very jubilant. They played on Mṛdaṅgas and Paṭahas.

4. After cutting off the head of Gaṇeśa even as Śiva became sorry, goddess Parvati became furious, O great sage.

5. "O what shall I do? Where shall I go? Alas, great misery has befallen me. How can this misery, this great misery be dispelled now?

6. "My son has been killed by all the gods and the Ganas. I shall destroy them all or create a deluge."

7. Lamenting thus, the great goddess of all the worlds angrily created in a moment hundreds and thousands of Saktis.

8. Saktis who were thus created, bowed to Parvati, the mother of the universe and blazing brilliantly spoke—"O mother, be pleased to command."

9. O great sage, on hearing that, Parvati, the Śakti of Śiva, the Prakṛti, the great Māyā, spoke to them all in great fury.

The goddess said:

10. O Saktis, O goddesses, now a great deluge shall be created by you at my bidding. You need not hesitate in this regard.

11. "O friends, devour forcibly all these sages, gods, Yakṣas, Rakṣasas belonging to us and others."

Brahmā said:

12. On being commanded by her, the infuriated Saktis got ready to destroy the gods and others.

13. Just as the fire consumes dry grass so also these Saktis attempted to destroy.

14-15. Leaders of Ganas or Viṣṇu, Brahmā or Śiva, Indra or Kubera, Skanda or the Sun—Saktis began to destroy them. Wherever one looked, Saktis were present.

16.   Karelis (the Terrific), Kubiaks (the humpbacked), Khañjās (the lame), Lambaśīrṣas (the tall-headed) the innumerable Śaktis took up the gods with their hands and threw them in their own mouths.

17-18. On seeing that Śiva, Brahmā, Viṣṇu, Indra, the other gods, Ganas and the sages began to doubt what the Goddess Parvati would be doing, whether she would create an untimely dissolution. Their hopes and aspirations for life were quelled.

19.   They all gathered together and discussed—"What shall be done now? Let us ponder." Discussing thus they spoke to one another.

20.   "Only when the goddess Parvati is pleased can there be a relief; not otherwise, even with our maximum efforts.

21.   Even Śiva who is an expert in different sports and is deluding us all, seems distressed like an ordinary man.

22.   When the hips of all the gods are broken and Parvati is fiery in rage, none of them dare stand before her.

23-24. Whether a person belonging to her or to others, whether a god, a demon, a Gaṇa, a guardian of the quarters, a Yakṣa, a Kinnara, a Sage, Brahmā, Viṣṇu or even lord Śiva himself, none could stand before Śiva.

25. On seeing her dazzling brilliance, burning all round, all of them were frightened and they stayed far away.

26. In the meantime, O sage Nārada, you of divine vision came there for the happiness of the gods and Ganas.

27. After bowing to me, Brahmā, Viṣṇu and Śiva and discussing jointly, he said—"Let us think and act together."

28. The gods then discussed with you of noble soul "How could our misery be quelled." They then said.

29. As long as the goddess Parvati does not favour us there will be no happiness. No suspicion need be entertained in this matter.

30. You and other sages went to Parvati in order to appease her anger. They then propitiated her.

31. They bowed to her again and again. They eulogised her with many hymns. They tried to please her with devotion and at the behest of the gods and Ganas spoke thus.

The celestial sages said:

32. O Mother of the universe, obeisance to you. Obeisance to you, O Śivā. Obeisance to you. O Caṇḍikā. Obeisance to you, Kalyani.

33. O mother, you alone are the primordial Śakti. You are the eternal cause of creation. You alone are the sustaining power. You alone are the cause of dissolution.

34. O goddess, be pleased. Spread peace. Obeisance be to you. O goddess, the three worlds are agitated by your fury.

Brahmā said:

35. The great goddess Parvati thus eulogised by you and other sages glanced at them furiously. She did not say anything.

36. Then the sages bowed at her lotus-like feet and spoke to her in low voice with devotion joining their palms in reverence.

The sages said:

37. O goddess, forgive, forgive. The final dissolution seems near at hand. Your lord is standing here. O mother, you see him.

38. What are we, the gods, Viṣṇu, Brahmā and others? We are only your subjects. We stand here with palms joined in reverence.

39. O great goddess, our guilts shall be forgiven. We are agitated and distressed. O Parvati give us peace.

Brahmā said:

40. After saying this, the agitated and distressed sages stood in front of her with palms joined in reverence.

41. On hearing their words Parvati was pleased and she replied to the sages with her mind full of compassion.

The goddess said:

42-43. If my son regains life and there may not be further annihilation. If you can arrange for him an honourable status and position among you as the chief presiding officer, there may be peace in the world. Otherwise you will never be happy.

Brahmā said:

44. Thus warned, you and other sages returned and intimated to all the gods everything in detail.

45. On hearing that, Indra and other gods joined their palms in reverence and piteously intimated to Śiva what had transpired there.

46. On hearing what the gods said, Śiva spoke thus— "It shall be done accordingly so that there may be peace over all the worlds."

47. "You shall go to the northern direction and whatever person you meet at first you cut off his head and fit it to this body."

Brahmā said:

48. Then they carried out Śiva's behests and acted accordingly. They brought the headless body of Gaṇeśa and washed it well.

49. They paid homage to it and started towards the north. It was a single-tusked elephant that they met.

50-51. They took the head and fitted it to the body. After joining it, the gods bowed to Śiva, Viṣṇu and Brahmā and spoke—"What has been ordered by you has been carried out by us. Let the task left incomplete be performed now."

52. Then the Pārṣadas shone happily. After hearing those words they awaited eagerly what Śiva would say.

53. Then Brahmā, Viṣṇu and other gods spoke after bowing to lord Śiva who is free from the ill effects of the attributes.

54. They said:—"Since we all are born out of your brilliant Energy let that Energy come into it by the recitation of the Vedic mantras.

55. Saying so, they jointly sprinkled the holy water, invoked by the mantras on that body after remembering Śiva.

56. Immediately after the contact of the holy water the boy was resuscitated to life and joined with consciousness. As Śiva willed, the boy woke up as from a sleep.

57. He was handsome, extremely comely. He had the face of an elephant. He was red-complexioned. He was delighted with face beaming. He was brilliant and had fine features.

58. O great sage, on seeing the son of Parvati resuscitated to life, they all rejoiced and their miseries came to an end.

59. They showed him delightfully to the goddess. On seeing her restored to life, the goddess was greatly delighted.

6.9 Ganesha crowned as the chief of Ganas (Chapter 18, Shiva Purana)

Nārada said:

1. O lord of subjects, when the son of Parvati was resuscitated and seen by the goddess, what happened then? Please narrate to me now.

Brahmā said:

2. O great sage, when the son of Parvati was resuscitated and seen by the goddess, listen to what happened there. I shall narrate the jubilation that ensued.

3. O sage, that son of Parvati was resuscitated. He was free from distress and perturbation. Then he was crowned by the gods and the leaders of Ganas.

4. On seeing her son, Parvati was highly delighted. Taking him up with both her hands she embraced him joyously.

5. She then lovingly gave him different clothes and ornaments.

6. He was honoured by the goddess who bestowed all Siddhis on him and touched him with her hand that removes all distress.

7. After worshipping her son, and kissing his face, she granted him boons with affection and said— "You have had great distress since your very birth."

8. You are blessed and contented now. You will receive worship before all the gods. You will be free from distress.

9. Vermillion is visible on your face now. Hence you will be worshipped with vermillion by all men always.

10-12. All achievements certainly accrue to him who performs your worship with flowers, sandal paste, scents, auspicious food offerings Nīrājana rites, betel leaves, charitable gifts, circumambulations and obeisance. All kinds of obstacles will certainly perish.

13. After saying this, she worshipped her good son with various articles, once again.

14. O Brahmin, then with the graceful blessings of Parvati, instantly peace-reigned upon gods and particularly on the Ganas.

15. In the meantime, Indra and other gods eulogised and propitiated Śiva joyously and brought him devoutly near Parvati.

16. After pleasing her they placed the boy in her lap for the happiness of the three worlds.

17. Placing his lotus-like hand on his head, Śiva told the gods. "This is another son of mine."

18-19. Getting up and bowing to Śiva, Parvati, Viṣṇu and me, Gaṇeśa stood in front of Nārada and other sages and said—"My guilt shall be forgiven. Arrogance is the characteristic of Man's nature."

20. We three Śiva, Viṣṇu and I said to the gods simultaneously with pleasure, after granting him excellent boons

21. "O great gods, just as we three are worshipped in all the three worlds, so also he shall be worshipped by all of you."

22. We are the off-springs of primordial nature. He is also the same and hence worthy of worship. He

is the remover of all obstacles and the bestower of the fruits of all rites.

23. He shall be worshipped first and we shall be worshipped afterwards. If he is not worshipped, we too are not worshipped.

24. If the other deities are worshipped when he is not worshipped, the fruit of that rite will be lost. There is no doubt in this matter.

25-26. After saying this we worshipped him. Śiva worshipped Gaṇeśa with various articles of worship. Viṣṇu worshipped him afterwards. I, Brahmā, and Parvati too worshipped him. He was then worshipped by all the gods and Ganas with great joy.

27. In order to gratify Parvati, Gaṇeśa was proclaimed as the presiding officer by all, Brahmā, Viṣṇu, Śiva and others.

28. Again, with a joyful mind, several boons were granted by Parvati to him, always favourable to all in the world.

Śiva said:

29. "O son of Parvati, I am pleased, there is no doubt about it. When I am pleased the entire universe is pleased. None will be against the same.

30. Since, even as a boy you showed great valour as Parvati's son, you will remain brilliant and happy always.

31. Let your name be the most auspicious in the matter of quelling obstacles. Be the presiding officer of all my Ganas and worthy of worship now."

32. After saying this, Śiva laid down several modes of worship and granted benedictions instantaneously.

33. The gods, the Ganas and the celestial damsels sang songs joyously, danced and played on instruments.

34. Another boon was granted to Gaṇeśa by the delighted Śiva of great soul.

35-37. O Gaṇeśa, you are born in the first Prahara on the fourth day in the dark half of the Bhadra mouth at the auspicious hour of the moonrise. Since your form manifested itself from the good mind of Parvati, your excellent Vrata shall be performed on that Tithi itself or beginning from that day. It will be very auspicious and conducive to the achievement of all Siddhis.

38. At the bidding of us both the Vrata shall be performed till the fourth day at the end of a year.

39. Let those who yearn for unequalled happiness in the world worship you devoutly in various ways on the fourth day in accordance with the rules.

40. On the fourth day of Lakshmi in the month of Margashirsha he shall perform early morning ablution and entrust the Vrata to the brahmins.

41. He shall perform worship with the Dūrvā grass and observe fast. After a Prahara has elapsed in the night the devotee shall take bath and worship.

42-43. The idol shall be made of metal, coral, white Arka flowers or clay. It shall be installed and worshipped by the devotee with all purity, with scents of various kinds, divine sandal paste and flowers.

44-45. A handful of Dūrvā grass having three knots and without roots shall be used for worship. The shoots shall be hundred and one in number. With twenty-one the idol shall be worshipped. Gaṇeśa shall be adored with incense, lamps and different kinds of food-offerings.

46. After worshipping you with various articles of worship like betel etc. and eulogising you with hymns, the devotee shall worship the crescent moon.

47. Afterwards, he shall feed the brahmins joyously with sweets with due honour. He himself shall take sweets and avoid salt.

48. Then the rites shall formally be dismissed. Then he shall remember Gaṇeśa. Thus the Vrata shall be concluded auspiciously.

49. When thus the Vrata is duly completed in a year, the devotee shall perform the rite of formal dismissal for the completion of the Vrata.

50. At my bidding twelve brahmins shall be fed. After placing a jar your image shall be worshipped.

51. After making the eight-petalled lotus diagram on the ground in accordance with Vedic injunctions a sacrifice shall be performed by the liberal people who have no disinclination to spend money.

52. Two women and two students shall be worshipped and fed in front of the idol duly.

53. The devotee shall keep awake at night and perform worship in the morning. After that the rites of formal dismissal with the mantra "Kṣemāya Punarāgamanāya Ca." (For welfare and return again) shall be performed.

54. The benediction as well as good wishes shall be received from the boy. In order to make the Vrata complete, handfuls of flowers shall be offered.

55. After prostrations, various routines shall be carried on. He who performs Vratas like this can secure the desired fruits.

56. O Gaṇeśa, he who performs your worship upto his ability, with faith, shall derive the fruit of all desires.

57. The devotee shall worship you, the lord of Gaṇas with vermillion, sandal paste, raw rice grains and Ketaka flowers as well as with other services.

58. They who devoutly worship you with acts of service will achieve success. Their obstacles will be quelled.

59. These Vratas shall be performed by the people of all castes, particularly by women as well as kings aiming and beginning to be prosperous and flourishing.

60. He will certainly derive whatever he desires. Hence you shall always be served by him whoever he is who desires fruits.

Brahmā said:

61-62. When this was mentioned by Śiva to Gaṇeśa of great soul, O sage, the gods, the sages and the Gaṇas, favourites of Śiva said "So be it" and worshipped Gaṇeśa according to prescribed rules.

63. All the Gaṇas, particularly bowed to Gaṇeśa and adored him respectfully with various articles.

64. O great sage, how can I describe even with my four mouths the indescribable delight of Parvati.

65. The divine drums were sounded. The celestial damsels danced. The Gandharva chiefs sang. Flowers were showered upon him.

66. When Gaṇeśa was installed, the whole universe attained peace and normalcy. There was great jubilation. All miseries ended.

67. O Nārada, Parvati and Śiva rejoiced in particular. Good and plentiful auspiciousness was conducive to happiness everywhere.

68-69. The gods and the sages, who had come there, returned at the bidding of Śiva praising Parvati and Gaṇeśa again and again, eulogising Śiva and saying "O what a battle!"

70. When Parvati became free from fury, Śiva and Parvati behaved as before.

71. With a desire for the welfare of the worlds, the great deity relaxing in his own soul and engaged in the activities of the devotees conferred different kinds of happiness.

72. Both Viṣṇu and I took leave of Śiva and after paying homage to both Parvati and Śiva returned to our abodes.

73. O holy sage Nārada, after singing the glory of Parvati and Śiva and taking leave of them you too returned to your abode.

74. Thus requested by you, I have narrated the glorious story of Parvati and Śiva along with that of Gaṇeśa with great reverence.

75. Whoever hears this narrative auspiciously with pure mind shall have everything auspicious and be the abode of auspiciousness.

76. The childless will get a son, the indigent wealth; the seeker of a wife will get a wife and the seeker of issues will get children.

77. The sick will regain health; the miserable will have good fortune. The sonless, impoverished, banished wife will be reunited with her husband.

78-79. The sorrowing will be relieved of sorrow, undoubtedly. The house that contains this story shall certainly be auspicious. He who listens to this narrative at the time of travel or on holy occasions, with a pure mind shall get all desires, thanks to the grace of lord Gaṇeśa.

SECTION 3:
GANESHA CONSCIOUSNESS

CHAPTER 7

GANESHA CONSCIOUSNESS

7.1 What is Consciousness?

The English word "conscious" originally derived from the Latin conscius (con- "together" and scio- "to know"), but the Latin word did not have the same meaning as the word -- it meant "knowing with", in other words "having joint or common knowledge with another". Google meaning of consciousness is: the fact of awareness by the mind of itself and the world. A man is distinguished above all animals by his self-consciousness, by which he is a 'rational animal'.

Consciousness is defined by some experts as the 'awareness of awareness' or self-awareness. According to Adi Shankara (700-750 CE), Consciousness is awareness, knowledge and intelligence. According to him, "Consciousness is Awareness of Reality" and "Awareness of Reality is Consciousness". The real experiencer is not the mind, but myself, the light in which everything appears. Self is the common factor at the root of all experience, the awareness in which everything happens. The entire field of consciousness is only as a film, or a speck, in 'I am'. This 'I am-ness' is, benign conscious of consciousness, being aware of itself. And it is indescribable, because it has no attributes. It is only being myself, and being myself is all that there is. Everything that exists, exists as myself.

7.1.1 Ancient Indian Hindu Perspectives about Consciousness

Perhaps the earliest known organized study of consciousness and of practices working with it can be traced to accounts of ancient Indian Hindu Vedic religion written in the Sanskrit language, thousands of years ago. Many would argue that never since has there been such detailed and elaborated activity on the part of human consciousness to understand itself and its relation to a larger context, where consciousness is presented as more central than material existence to the nature, composition, and processes comprising all of reality. One might even venture to say that this Vedic period was the high point to date in human history with regard to our study of the nature of consciousness and the ways with which it may be worked.

From the point of view of Indian tradition, there have emerged multi-level cosmological models that provide structural frameworks to understand the relationship between consciousness and creativity.

Among them is pancha kosha (from Sanskrit –pancha means five, and kosha means sheath) encompassing five bodies (koshas) of consciousness:

(i) Annamaya Kosha (food body/physical body),

(ii) Pranamaya Kosha (vital sheath/prana/life force),

(iii) Manomaya Kosha (the emotional body/mind),

(iv) Vijnanamaya (cognition/ intellect/wisdom), and

(v) Anandamaya (bliss), considered the "most useful springboard for a modern scientific understanding of cosmology and evolution".

This description of the human body in terms of pancha kosha is described in Taittiriya Upanishad, an ancient scripture in Hinduism. The anandamaya kosha is the subtlest causal level, so subtle that it "touches" and partakes of the nature of the spirit self. Functionally speaking, it is a mixture of subtle energy and pure consciousness–though it is not really, since "beyond all sheaths is the Self." (Taittiriya Upanishad 2:5:2b). Anandamaya is the self that discovers or rather realizes itself in ecstasy, in a consciousness charged with delight. It is therefore that beauty and harmony of the world become the perennial source of happiness and freedom and draw out of the human being the deepest of cognitive and moral impulses. Anandamaya kosha, the blissful sheath, is the most interior of the kosha, the first of the koshas surrounding the Atman, the eternal centre of consciousness, the central, formless, imperceptible, unknowable, illumined spiritual Self, or Atman, or soul.

First, we know the Self–the individual Self, the jivatman–and then we are enabled to know the Supreme Self, the Paramatman: Brahman. And the Self we will know is itself , with the following attributes:

(i) **Immutable.** Eternally changeless, incapable of being either diminished or increased, for it is one with the Infinite.

(ii) **Pure.** Ever only itself, never really being influenced or changed by anything whatsoever. Untainted by any contact, for it is untouchable.

(iii) **Shadowless.** The Self is Pure Light within which there is no shadow of darkness or differentiation. It is always exactly what it is.

(iv) **Bodiless.** It is perfectly non-dual. It is neither inside or outside of anything. It cannot be contained. It is absolutely one, having nothing appended to it or necessary to it.

(v) **Colourless.** It has no "qualities" or "characteristics" but is always 'I AM'. The three gunas are not present in it, nor are any gradations of any kind. It is indescribable. All we can really say about it is what it is not. All of these terms indicate that the Self is the same as Brahman. And the Self that knows its Self– Brahman, "wherein live the mind, the senses, the pranas, the elements"–does in truth come to know all things and the Self in all things.

(vi) **Omniscience and omnipresence** are experienced by that liberated spirit who knows its oneness with 'The All'.

Atman in Sanskrit literature means "real self" of the individual, "innermost essence", and soul. Atman, in

Hinduism, is considered as eternal, imperishable, beyond time, "not the same as body or mind or consciousness, but is something beyond which permeates all these". In Advaita (nondual) Vedanta, it is "pure, undifferentiated, self-shining consciousness," the witness-consciousness which observes all phenomena yet is not touched by it.

The Mandukya Upanishad, speaking of the consciousness of the self, or turiya, describes it as "not subjective experience, nor objective experience, nor experience intermediate between these two, nor is it a negative condition which is neither consciousness nor unconsciousness. It is not the knowledge of the senses, nor is it relative knowledge, nor yet inferential knowledge. Beyond the senses, beyond the understanding, beyond all expression. It is pure unitary consciousness, wherein awareness of the world and of multiplicity is completely obliterated. It is ineffable peace. It is the supreme good. It is One without a second. It is the Self. Know it alone!" Who can say any more?

Mandukya Upanishad goes further and asks: What am I then? The limitless 'I'. And what is the limitless 'I'? The limitless 'I' is called the substrate in Vedanta. A substrate makes the error that 'I' is limited possible. The rope in our example, is a substrate, something whose nature is so subtle that it is possible to mistake it for something else, like a snake in the dark. The fact that I'm formless Consciousness makes the playing of myriad roles possible. This Upanishad concludes, 'I' am infinite non-dual pure Consciousness. Because I am other than the body. I don't suffer its changes. I am neither born nor do I die. I have no sense organs. So, I am uninvolved in the world. Because I am other than the mind, I am free from sorrow, attachment, malice and fear. Scripture says I am pure, without thought and desire and so I am. I have no attributes. I live without breathing. I am eternal, formless and ever-free. I am the same in all, filling all things with being. I am infinite non-dual pure Consciousness.

In a flawless crystal, what do we see? Nothing. So also, in the self there is nothing seen, because all the "things" are transcended, and pure Being alone remains in our consciousness. Wherefore the Chandogya Upanishad tells us: "Where one sees nothing but the One, hears nothing but the One, knows nothing but the One—there is the Infinite. Where one sees another, hears another, knows another—there is the finite. The Infinite is immortal, the finite is mortal."

The unwitnessed witness is the self. In truth there is no other witness on the individual level because the senses, mind, and intellect are mere energy constructs that have no consciousness of their own. The eye never really sees, nor does the ear hear. No more does the brain or intellect. Rather, the spirit that is consciousness witnesses their messages, therefore the Upanishadic seer said: "The Self is ear of the ear, mind of the mind, speech of speech. He is also breath of the breath, and eye of the eye. Having given up the false identification of the Self with the senses and the mind, and knowing the Self to be Brahman, the wise, on departing this life, become immortal." The Self is the source of all light–the Inner Light of Consciousness that illumines all things. For outside the Self there is no perception of even the brightest of material suns. It is the presence of the Self that produces awareness of all phenomena. Outside the Self nothing at all exists. Within the Self is everything. Nothing of heaven or earth illumines the Self or causes It to be radiant. Rather, It is swayam-prakash: self-luminous. Furthermore, it is the Self that illumines all beings. "He is the one light that gives light to all." The Self is the essential nature of all sentient beings that "shine" with consciousness.

According to Chapter 13, Verse 34 in Bhagavad Gita, Lord Krishna says to Arjuna, "O son of Bharata, as the sun alone illuminates all this universe, so does the living entity, one within the body, illuminate the entire body by consciousness."

Correct understanding of Advaita Vedanta is believed to provide knowledge of one's true identity as Ātman, the dispassionate and unchanging witness-consciousness, and the identity of Ātman and Brahman, which results in liberation. This is achieved through what Adi Shankara refers to as anubhava, immediate intuition, a direct awareness which is construction-free, and not construction-filled. It is not an awareness of Brahman, but instead an awareness that is Brahman.

The main question here is the relation between Atman and Brahman, which is solved by regarding them to be identical. This truth is established from the oldest

Principal Upanishads and Brahma Sutras, and is also found in parts of the Bhagavad Gitā and numerous other Hindu texts, and is regarded to be self-evident. The main aim of the commentaries is to support this nondualistic (of Atman and Brahman) reading of the sruti. Reason is being used to support revelation, the sruti, the ultimate source of truth.

7.2 Consciousness and Non-Dualism

Atman (soul) is a key topic of the Upanishads, but they express two distinct, somewhat divergent themes. Some teach that Brahman (highest reality; universal principle; *'sat-chit-anand'* or 'being-consciousness-bliss') is identical with Atman, while others teach that Atman is part of Brahman but not identical to it. This ancient debate flowered into various dual and non-dual theories in Hinduism. The Brahmasutra by Badarayana (~100 BCE) synthesized and unified these somewhat conflicting theories, stating that Atman and Brahman are different in some respects, particularly during the state of ignorance, but at the deepest level and in the state of self-realization, Atman and Brahman are identical, non-different, non-dual (advaita). This synthesis overcame the dualistic tradition of Samkhya-Yoga schools and realism-driven traditions of Nyaya-Vaiseshika schools, enabling it to become the foundation of Vedanta as Hinduism's enduring spiritual tradition.

7.2.1 Non-duality in Hinduism

In spirituality, nondualism, also called non-duality, means "not two" or "one undivided without a second". "Advaita" is from Sanskrit roots a, not; dvaita, dual, and is usually translated as "nondualism", "nonduality" and "nondual". Nondualism primarily refers to a mature state of consciousness, in which the dichotomy of I-other is "transcended", and awareness is described as "centerless" and "without dichotomies". Although this state of consciousness may seem to appear spontaneous, it usually follows prolonged preparation through ascetic or meditative/contemplative practice, which may include ethical injunctions. When referring to nondualism, Hinduism generally uses the Sanskrit term Advaita, while Buddhism uses Advaya (Tibetan: gNis-med, Chinese: pu-erh, Japanese: fu-ni). While the term "nondualism" is derived from Advaita Vedanta, descriptions of nondual consciousness can be found within Hinduism (Turiya, sahaja), Buddhism (emptiness, pariniṣpanna, nature of mind, rigpa), Sufism (Wahdat al Wujud, Fanaa, and Haqiqah) and western Christian and neo-Platonic traditions (henosis, mystical union).

The oldest surviving manuscript on Advaita Vedanta is by Gauḍapada (6th century CE), who has traditionally been regarded as the teacher of Govinda Bhagavatpada and the grand teacher of Adi Shankara. Advaita is best known from the Advaita Vedanta tradition of Adi Shankara (788-820 CE), who states that Brahman, the single unified eternal truth, is pure Being, Consciousness and Bliss (Sat-chit-ananda).

Correct understanding of Advaita Vedanta is believed to provide knowledge of one's true identity as Ātman, the dispassionate and unchanging witness-consciousness, and the identity of Ātman and Brahman, which results in liberation. This is achieved through what Adi Shankara refers to as anubhava, immediate intuition, a direct awareness which is construction-free, and not construction-filled. It is not an awareness of Brahman, but instead an awareness that is Brahman.

The main question here is the relation between Atman and Brahman, which is solved by regarding them to be identical. This truth is established from the oldest Principal Upanishads and Brahma Sutras, and is also found in parts of the Bhagavad Gitā and numerous other Hindu texts, and is regarded to be self-evident. The main aim of the commentaries is to support this nondualistic (of Atman and Brahman) reading of the sruti. Reason is being used to support revelation, the sruti, the ultimate source of truth.

The Asian ideas of nondualism developed in the Vedic and post-Vedic Upanishadic philosophies as well as in the Buddhist traditions. The oldest traces of nondualism in Indian thought are found in the earlier Hindu Upanishads such as Brihadaranyaka Upanishad, as well as other pre-Buddhist Upanishads such as the Chandogya Upanishad, which emphasizes the unity of individual soul called Atman and the Supreme Soul, called Brahman. In Hinduism, nondualism has more commonly become associated with the Advaita Vedanta tradition of Adi Shankara.

According to Verse 4.3.32 of the Brihadaranyaka Upanishad (~800 BCE),

An ocean is that one seer, without any duality (Advaita); this is the Brahma-world, O King. Thus, did Yajnavalkya teach him. This is his highest goal, this is his highest success, this is his highest world, this is his highest bliss. All other creatures live on a small portion of that bliss.

—Brihadaranyaka Upanishad 4.3.32

Just as the cosmos is an extension of the Consciousness that is Brahman, in the same way our

individual prana is an extension of our Self (atman). It is inseparable from the Self because it is the Self. This is the authentic non-duality (Advaita) of the Upanishads, not a negation or denial of either Prakriti or prana. Seeing them as separate from Spirit, and therefore dual, is the error—not acknowledging their intimate reality.

In the Upanishads, which teach a doctrine that has been interpreted in a nondualistic way, mainly *'tat tvam asi'*. The Advaita Vedanta of Shankara, which teaches that a single pure consciousness is the only reality, and that the world is unreal (Maya). Non-dual forms of Hindu Tantra including Kashmira Shaivism and the goddess-centred

Shaktism highlight this concept. Their view is similar to Advaita, but they teach that the world is not unreal, but it is the real manifestation of consciousness.

The philosophy of Recognition, as outlined by thinkers like Utpaladeva of Kashmir Shaivism, teaches that though the identity of all souls is one with God (Isvara) or Shiva (which is the single reality, Being and absolute consciousness), they have forgotten this due to Maya or ignorance. However, through knowledge one can recognize one's authentic divine nature and become a liberated being. Another important element of Trika theology is the active and dynamic nature of consciousness, which is described as the spontaneous vibration or pulsation (spanda) of universal consciousness, which is an expression of its freedom (svātāntrya) and power (Śakti). Because of this, though this philosophy is idealist, it affirms the reality of the world and everyday life, as a real transformation (parinama), manifestation or appearance (ābhāsa) of the absolute consciousness. The Absolute is also explained through the metaphor of light (prakasha) and reflective awareness (vimarsha).

According to Non-duality in Kashmir (Trika) Shaivism, all that exists, throughout all time and beyond, is one infinite divine Consciousness, free and blissful, which projects within the field of its awareness a vast multiplicity of apparently differentiated subjects and objects: each object an actualization of a timeless potentiality inherent in the Light of Consciousness, and each subject the same plus a contracted locus of self-awareness. This creation, a divine play, is the result of the natural impulse within Consciousness to express the totality of its self-knowledge in action, an impulse arising from love. The unbounded Light of Consciousness contracts into finite embodied loci of awareness out of its own free will. When those finite subjects then identify with the limited and circumscribed cognitions and circumstances that make up this phase of their existence, instead of identifying with the transindividual overarching pulsation of pure Awareness that is their true nature, they experience what they call "suffering." To rectify this, some feel an inner urge to take up the path of spiritual gnosis and yogic practice, the purpose of which is to undermine their misidentification and directly reveal within the immediacy of awareness the fact that the divine powers of Consciousness, Bliss, Willing, Knowing, and Acting comprise the totality of individual experience as well—thereby triggering a recognition that one's real identity is that of the highest Divinity, the Whole in every part. This experiential gnosis is repeated and reinforced through various means until it becomes the nonconceptual ground of every moment of experience, and one's contracted sense of self and separation from the Whole is finally annihilated in the incandescent radiance of the complete expansion into perfect wholeness. Then one's perception fully encompasses the reality of a universe dancing ecstatically in the animation of its completely perfect divinity.

This single supreme reality is also sometimes referred to as Aham (the heart). It is considered to be a non-dual interior space of Śiva, support for the entire manifestation, supreme mantra and identical to Śakti. In Kashmir Shivaism the highest form of Kali is Kalasankarshini who is Nirguna, formless and is often show as a flame above the head of Guhya Kali the highest gross form of Kali. In Nepali Newar arts, both form and formless attributes of Kali is often envisioned in a single art form showing the hierarchy of goddesses in their tradition. In it Guhya kali image culminates in flame, with Kalasankarshini, the highest deity in the sequence, who consumes time within herself and is envisioned solely as a flame representing Para Brahman.

Advaita appears in different shades in various schools of Hinduism such as in Advaita Vedanta, Vishishtadvaita Vedanta (Vaishnavism), Suddhadvaita Vedanta (Vaishnavism), non-dual Shaivism and Shaktism. In the Advaita Vedanta of Adi Shankara, advaita implies that all of reality is one with Brahman, that the Atman (soul, self) and Brahman (ultimate unchanging reality) are one. Philosophical schools such as Advaita (non-dualism) see the "spirit/soul/self" within each living entity as being fully identical with Brahman. The Advaita school believes that there is one soul that connects and exists in all the living beings, regardless of their shapes or forms, and there is no distinction, no superior, no inferior, no separate devotee soul (Atman), no separate God soul (Brahman). This oneness unifies all beings, there is a divine in every being, and that all existence is a single reality, state the Advaita Vedanta Hindus. Advaita Vedanta philosophy considers Atman as self-existent awareness, limitless and non-dual. To Advaitins, the Atman is the Brahman, the Brahman is the Atman, each self is non-different from the infinite. Atman is the universal principle, one eternal undifferentiated self-luminous consciousness, the truth asserts Advaita Hinduism. Human beings, in a state of unawareness of this universal self, see their "I-ness" as different from the being in others, then act out of impulse, fears, cravings, malice, division, confusion, anxiety, passions, and a sense of distinctiveness. To Advaitins, Atman-knowledge is the state of full awareness, liberation, and freedom that overcomes dualities at all levels, realizing the divine within oneself, the divine in others, and in all living beings; the non-dual oneness, that God is in everything, and everything is God. This identification of individual living beings/souls, or jivatmas, with the 'one Atman' is the non-dualistic Advaita Vedanta position.

7.3 What is Ganesha Consciousness?

Ganesha consciousness is a state of awareness in which an individual acts in complete harmony with the Divine or the ultimate reality of Ganesha. It is a form of Bhakti yoga (or devotional service) in which the purpose is to devote one's thoughts, actions and worship to pleasing Ganesha, who some consider to be the supreme god.

To act with Ganesha consciousness is to free the self from the illusion that it is an individual body. It is a way to experience the bliss of one's true, eternal nature. It is said that anyone can do this and that Ganesha consciousness is something everyone has naturally.

Ganesha consciousness can be reawakened through Bhakti yoga practices such as hearing and chanting about Ganesha. This process brings love (bhakti), which attracts Ganesha and allows the devotee to develop their own unique relationship with Him.

Ganesha Consciousness is the preeminent consciousness of all Divine Archetypes. It is beyond Time and Space, capable of the greatest intelligence and wisdom, and unlimited in its ability to do anything:

- Time/space mastery equal to Kalabhairava;

- Protection equivalent of Vishnu;

- Wealth equivalent to Lakshmi;

- Purity equal to Shiva;

- Wisdom equal to Murugan;

- Intelligence equal to Saraswati,

- Compassion and power equivalent to Shakti;

- Mind/body/soul strength equivalent to Hanuman.

What sets Ganesha apart from all other Archetypes is his ability to give results faster. It's because of his special intelligence to see every shortcut and remove any obstacles, traits only Ganesha has!

7.4 Lord Ganesha, the powerful God of Prosperity and Intelligence

Ganesha offers prosperity and success to all who invoke him. As Lord of Beginnings and the Remover of Obstacles, he's the first to call on before the undertaking of a new task or business.

His large head personifies knowledge and intelligence. Ganesha's small eyes represent keen, precise observation. He reminds us to focus our attention on the workings of our own mind, watch how it runs here and there, never immobile, a continuous flow of unceasing thoughts. Ganesha worship can bestow both siddhi (success), buddhi (intellect) and riddhi (wealth). Because of his power of buddhi (intelligence), he is also revered in Buddhism and Jainism.

The Ganapati Upanishad asserts that Ganesha is same as the ultimate reality, Brahman. This is put in practice by the Ganapatya sect.

Ganesha worship leads to self-purification as Ganesha removes the obstacles of ignorance, delusion, attachments and egoism from his devotees. The real obstacles are those that clog our minds and prevent us from seeing and discerning truth or reality. Lord Ganesha helps us see the truth which is hidden in all.

Fear is the most formidable obstacle in our lives. Ganesha frees our minds from fear and also strengthens our resolve and courage. With Ganesha worship, devotees can overcome fear and gain strength and courage to realize their goals.

Ganesha reigns over muladhara chakra. He is the ruler of both the instinctive mind and of the intellectual mind. He clears the mind so that awareness can flow into it.

7.4.1 Attributes of Ganesha: From Form to Formlessness (Consciousness)

Ganesha is actually a consciousness. For the convenience of worshippers, it is shown in the real form. Every body part of Ganesha's representation teaches us something of deep spiritual significance:

- **Small Eyes** symbolize concentration. Ganesha's eyes teach us to concentrate our mind, as only a person who has controlled his mind can achieve any success in life.

- **Big Head** — symbolizes Ganesha as the god of Wisdom. His elephant head indicates intelligence and discrimination.

- **Big Ears** — that means 'listen more'. Ganesha's wide ears denote the ability to listen to people who seek his help. Ears are also used to gain knowledge.

- **Small Mouth** — that means 'talk less' and value our words.

- **Big Belly** — Digest all good and bad in life, and you will attain the virtue of calmness. Ganesha's belly contains infinite universes; this signifies the ability of Ganesha to swallow the sorrows of the universe and protect the world.

- **Blessing Hand** — The third hand, turned towards the devotee, is in a pose of blessing. Ganesha offers protection and guidance to the spiritual seeker. We must also offer that same grace and blessings to those we meet on the path of life.

- **Four Arms** — represent the four cardinal directions and his mastery over the physical world (similar to how Lord Brahma has four heads).

- **Mark on the Forehead** — Ganesha's urdha mark signifies being a Master of Time. On Ganesha's forehead is located the trishula, symbolizing Time (past, present, and future) and Ganesha's mastery over it.

- **Axe** — represents the severing of all bonds, attachments and desires, and therefore of pain and suffering.

- **Sweets** — The fourth hand holds modaka (sweets), which symbolizes the reward of sadhana (devotion).

7.4.2 The Ashtavinayaka: Eight Manifestations of Lord Ganesha

The Ashtavinayaka, or Eight Forms of Lord Ganesha are mentioned in the Mudgala Purana, which is consecrated exclusively to Him. In each form, he defeats each of the eight human weaknesses:

- **Vakratunda** (defeats Matsaryasura, the demon of jealousy and envy)

- **Ekadanta** (defeats Madasura, the demon of arrogance)

- **Mahodara** (defeats Mohasura, the demon of confusion and delusion)

- **Gajanana (or Gajavaktra)** (defeats Lobhasura, the demon of greed)

- **Lambodara** (defeats Krodhasura, the demon of anger)

- **Vikata** (defeats Kamasura, the demon of lust)

- **Vighnaraja** (defeats Mamasura, the demon of ego and possessiveness)

- **Dhumravarna** (defeats Abhimanasura, the demon of self-infatuation, pride and attachment)

7.5 Ganesha is Consciousness

I am Ganesha. I am your Consciousness. I am the actions that you do consciously, knowingly. I am the child, the off-spring of The Divine Father and The Divine Mother

– your Unconscious and the Subconscious. On a higher level, I am the Universal Consciousness – the inter-connectedness of the universe. Since I am in one and all – the plants, the animals and the humans – I connect you all to one another. I am The Divine Connection. I represent non-duality. I am the Universal Conscious Feeling. Just like my Divine Parents – I am all pervading. I am Ganesha. I am your conscious Guide. I am The Force, The Power in you that lets you know – that lets you be aware of the universe; of what is happening all around you, in you and outside you.

7.5.1 How can you know me (Ganesha)?

By consciously being aware of yourself. The more conscious you are, the more in tune with me you are. When you are about to do something and are aware of the consequences – you are witnessing me. Since I am your Guide (whether you let me be or not , I AM THAT), I make you aware of the result, in your consciousness. Some stop themselves (when the action is negative) and some still go ahead. But my constant presence is always there.

Without The Divine Unconscious & The Subconscious, I cannot exist. I am

7.5.2 The Third of The Divine Trinity

Because of me, Ganesha – The Universal Consciousness, actions of a person in this corner of the world affect the persons in the other, faraway corner of the world. This is called "Universal Entanglement". The power to stop yourself or to go ahead, is unique to humans. That is the Divine Choice residing in you – The Power of Viveka – to be able to sift and sort in your mind and then make a choice.

I am The Voice of Wisdom in you – your Divine Guide. I am the Power of Clarity because having sifted and sorted, what remains, what comes out is – Light out of darkness. I am the Harbinger of light in your life.

I am the Courage in you – The Power that sees you through difficult times and brings out the victorious in you.

I am The Conscious Joy that you feel. The joy that you feel on accomplishing your goals – That is Ganesha. The joy that you feel when you help someone – That is Ganesha. The joy that you feel when you know in your heart that you have done the right thing – That is Ganesha.

Just be in observance of your life – and you can witness my glory.

I am Ganesha – your Friend.

SECTION 4:
SCIENCE OF GANESHA CONSCIOUSNESS

CHAPTER 8

SCIENCE OF GANESHA CONSCIOUSNESS

8.1 Science of Ganesha Consciousness

Hinduism now stands as the religion of the village community as well as the urban family, an enlightened faith for all men in all times. The single most unifying force within Hinduism is Lord Ganesha, son of Siva-Shakti, beloved Deity of 900 million Hindus.

To Him we offer our reverent love and praise. It is an incontrovertible fact that Lord Ganesha is real, not a mere symbol. He is a potent force in the universe, not a representation of potent universal forces. Corpulently built, Lord Ganesha is said to contain within Himself all matter, all mind. He is the very personification of material existence. We look upon this physical world as the body of Lord Ganesha. In seeing and understanding the varied forces at work in the physical universe, we are seeing and understanding the powers and the being of Lord Ganesha. There is nothing that happens on this material plane of existence except that it is the will of God Shiva and minutely detailed by His beloved son Lord Ganesha. When this is known, life becomes a daily joyous experience, for we know that all that happens , whether it brings sorrow or happiness, whether we personally wanted it to happen or not, still we know that all that happens, is right and good, for it flowed from the wisdom and benevolent kindness of our loving Ganesha, the gracious Lord of Dharma. This wonderful spirit all Hindus strives to carry into daily life, a complete trust that all that happens is for the best, a full knowing that the Supreme God's will prevails everywhere and that the elephant-faced God is caring for each detail every minute of every hour of the day.

Hinduism is at the heart of science, and yet its understanding of the universe lies beyond the most advanced scientist's conceptualization. Modern science, like the Vedic rishis, describes the whole of the universe as energy in one form or another. Matter itself is merely condensed energy, as Einstein's renowned equation, $E=MC2$, proclaims in mystic brevity.

8.2 A Meditation on the Gods and Three Types of Forces of Energy

There are three strong forces at work in the universe: **gravity, electromagnetism and the nuclear force.** In the following, we offer a meditation comparing these three energies that are affecting our lives all the time to the powers of Lord Ganesha, Lord Murugan and God Shiva. It is a general analogy — not meant to be theologically perfect — humbly offered as an aid to understanding the unique characteristics of the Deities.

We can then liken His nature to the force of gravity, as one gravitational pull in one part of the universe affects all other parts of the universe that very instant, no matter how distant. The nine planets in this solar system affect all humans and plants in their interaction, so precise is Ganesha's mind, the Lord of Karma, the Lord of Dharma.

If you forge ahead for a good cause, even when all the forces of the universe align themselves against you, including society itself, you will succeed. It's a little like a great elephant walking through the forest, clearing all barriers for those who follow. Such blessings come to those who follow Ganesha. Slowly the forces will clear, and all benefit from His grace.

8.2.1 Gravitational Force

Tradition describes the entire universe as being contained in Lord Ganesha's big belly. Thus we look upon Him in this meditation as the overlord who holds sway over the material universe, the sum of cosmic mass. And one of His potencies is gravity. Gravity is a mysterious force to the scientist even today. It is the galactic glue that draws and holds larger mass together and gives order to the macrocosm. It is an instantaneous force, so that when one celestial body moves in a remote corner of a galaxy, all other masses throughout the galaxy adjust simultaneously, even though it would take light, at its incredible speed, millions of years to travel the distance. This implies to the scientist what the Hindu knew from the beginning, that space and time are relative concepts and there is a "something" that exists everywhere in the universe at once. Like gravity, Lord Ganesha is totally predictable and known for orderliness. Without gravity, the known galactic systems could not exist. Masses would stray apart; all organization of life as we know it, would be impossible. Gravity is the basis of ordered existence in the macrocosm, and our loving Ganesha holds dominion over its mysteries.

8.2.2 Electromagnetic Force

Within and between the atoms that comprise our physical universe there reigns a second force: electromagnetism. Lord Murugan, Kartikeya, holds sway over the forces which bind sub-atomic particles together. (Note: Kartikeya, also known as Skanda, Kumara, Murugan and Subrahmanya, is the Hindu god of war. He is a son of Parvati and Shiva, brother of Ganesha, and a god whose life story has many versions in Hinduism. An important deity in the Indian subcontinent since ancient times, Kartikeya is particularly popular and predominantly worshipped in South India, Sri Lanka, Singapore and Malaysia as Murugan.)

The electromagnetic force is many magnitudes greater than the gravitational force, but because it works in the microcosm of existence, it has less influence on our daily lives than the gravitational force. Similarly, Ganesha is more involved in our day-to-day concerns than is Lord Murugan, whose power is electric, given more to change than to order, more to the unsuspected than to the predictable. Like the powerful forces that bind together the atomic systems of protons, neutrons, electrons, quanta, quarks and other sub-atomic "particles," Lord Murugan's shakti works deeply within us, within our spiritual sphere, within the great depths of the mind. His electric power issues forth from the shakti vel. Just as the energy races through the universe in the form of radio, radar and light waves, x-rays, heat, gamma and cosmic rays, so does Murugan's electric shakti impacts our life. Just as we experience light and darkness, positive and negative potential, so do the electromagnetic forces issue forth from Murugan's realm of positive and negative forces, of devas and their asuric counterparts.

Like gravity, Lord Ganesha is always with us, supporting and guiding our physical existence. And just like electrostatic energy, Lord Murugan is most often invisible, working in a sphere of which we are not always conscious, present in our lives through His radiant energies and light, yet not so apparently known as Lord Ganesha. The ancient Agamas offer a more philosophically technical summary of the above. They declare that Ganesha rules over ashuddha maya, the gross energies of the odic realms from the thirteenth tattva to the 36th. Murugan's domain, they state, is shuddhashuddha maya, the realms of actinodic energy, being the sixth to the twelfth tattvas. Finally, they declare that Shiva's domain is shuddha maya, the purely spiritual realms of actinic energy, being the first to the fifth tattvas in the unfolding of the universe.

8.2.3 Atomic or Nuclear Energy

God, Shiva, is the Lord of Lords and the source of all energies in the universe. His is the most interior sphere of all — the nuclear energies within sub-atomic particles and the essence even of that. Of all energies, the nuclear energy is by far the most powerful; and of all the Hindu Gods, God Shiva reigns supreme. At the core of matter, Lord Shiva whirls through His Cosmic Dance as Nataraja. Never has a greater conception been seen by seers to describe the divine operations of the universe. We quote from the book, The Tao of Physics, by noted physicist and researcher Fritjof Capra:

"The dance of Siva is the dancing universe; the ceaseless flow of energy going through an infinite variety of patterns that melt into one another. Modern physics has shown that the rhythm of creation and destruction is not only manifest in the turn of the seasons and in the birth and death of all living creatures, but is also the very essence of inorganic matter. According to quantum field theory, all interactions between the constituents of matter take place through the emission and absorption of virtual particles. More than that, the dance of creation and destruction is the basis of the very existence of matter, since all material particles 'self-interact' by emitting and reabsorbing virtual particles. Modern physics has thus revealed that every subatomic particle not only performs an energy dance, but also is an *energy dance, a pulsating process of creation and destruction. For the modern physicist, then, Shiva's* dance is the dance of subatomic matter, a continual dance of creation and destruction involving the whole cosmos, the basis of existence and of all natural phenomena. The metaphor of the Cosmic Dance thus unifies ancient mythology, religious art and modern physics. It is indeed, as Coomaraswamy has said, 'poetry, but science nonetheless."

8.3 Hinduism's Unsurpassed Cosmology

Hindus may be justifiably proud of a religion which postulated thousands of years ago a cosmology that only today is being discovered and appreciated by science through the ponderous process of reason and empirical proof. Hinduism knew the truth of the source and organization of the universe long before Newton and Einstein confirmed the validity of our world view. While many Western religious systems stand opposed to science or alter their beliefs according to its evolving conclusions, it is one of the great heritages of the Hindu perception of the all-pervasive God, soul and cosmos that we have spiritual Truths that are in complete accord with and cannot be refuted by modern science.

Consciousness and its Quantum Characteristics

If we polish our world-view lens with a coating of

quantum consciousness,

we shall be able to leapfrog our creativity and

concept of the inner world.

8.4 Brief (non-mathematical) Introduction of Quantum Mechanics

Quantum Mechanics brings science face-to-face with metaphysics, and that is incongruent with unpleasant to some of the scientists, considering the manner in which they conduct 21st century science. However, as we shall see shortly that the concept of quantum physics and consciousness is inescapable if we wish appreciate metaphysics and realise the bliss of life in the true sense. So, let us begin introducing quantum mechanics from the point of a layman.

Picture the nucleus of an atom in the centric position of our sun. According to Bohr's model of the atom, the nucleus is positively charged and composed of neutral particles called neutrons and positively-charged protons. The neutrons and protons are made up of subatomic "particles" known as quarks, leptons and bosons; however, these subclasses are not immediately pertinent to our discussions here. The positive charge of the protons in the nucleus is balanced to neutrality by an appropriate number of electrons spinning around the nucleus, much the way the planets in our solar system revolve about our sun.

8.4.1 What is Quantum?

A quantum is a discrete packet of energy, proposed for the first time by Max Planck, in 1900. It denotes that the energy exchange between the two bodies can take place in terms discrete quanta (plural of quantum) of light-one quantum, two quanta, three quanta, etc., but never half quantum and never continuous exchange of energy. One quantum of radiation of energy is one photon. The energy carried by a photon is directly proportional to the frequency associated with it,

The electrons revolving about the nucleus of the atom can increase or decrease their energy levels (orbits) by interaction with a variety of forces, including photons of appropriate energy. For example, a low energy electron circumnavigating the nucleus in say a "Mercury" orbit close to the "solar nucleus" can be excited or stimulated by a number of methods with an appropriately energetic photon to "jump" to a higher energy orbit, say the "Jupiter" orbit. Or the reverse can occur, an electron can "jump" from the "Jupiter" orbit down to the lower energy "Mercury" orbit with a consequent emission of energy, usually in the form of a photon. Using this model, often called the "Old Quantum Mechanics," we can derive and describe a number of useful conclusions based on the laws of quantum mechanics, which in more than 100 years have never made a wrong prediction.

But to dig deeply into the metaphysics of quantum theory, we must make the transition to the New Quantum Mechanics, as developed in the mid-1920s by Werner Heisenberg, Erwin Schrödinger, and other astute theoreticians. We will describe both of these models a bit later. However, a word of caution and clarity–despite the practical effectiveness of quantum mechanical models, most physicists believe that atoms, electrons, neutrons and protons are not solid particles, as these models might imply. They are more precisely, packets of information and energy. That being said, quantum mechanics can explain numerous properties of what we, with our five senses, perceive to be the stuff of our universe. More important, and perhaps quite surprising, it can provide you with a more accurate perspective of your true reality, and thereby give you specific tools that can significantly enhance your quality of life and well-being. As we shall see, this is by no means any kind of "hocus pocus," but is based on the proven results and implications of experiments and models at the interface of quantum physics and our true reality.

In all that follows, almost no mathematics and only elementary concepts in physics will be used

We will touch on the following *profound phenomena.* They are derived directly from quantum theory:

8.4.2 Quantum Jumps

In an atom, negatively-charged electrons can be considered to be whirling about the atom's positively-charged nucleus, occupying different energy levels or orbits. There are many ways to stimulate an electron to jump from one energy level or orbit to another, either to a higher or lower level. This movement is called a "quantum jump." In the process, the electron is initially present at say energy level 1, and then jumps to energy level 2. Before and after the jump, it can be observed at each of these respective energy levels. However, during the quantum jump process, it exists nowhere in between. Quantum mechanics forbids its existence between the levels.

8.4.3 Electron's Probability of Location

The electrons around the immediate diameter of an atom spend more than 95 percent of their time within a tight radius about the nucleus. However, there is a small, but finite probability that these electrons can be found anywhere in the universe. Technically speaking, we are all intimately sharing our electrons with each other, and in fact with all matter in the universe. There is a probability of electron contact with everyone from Joe Biden to a gorilla in Uganda!

8.4.4 Observer Effect

What you perceive as your reality is actually something you create by your observation of the universe. When you"consciously" observe something under a given set of circumstances, an event occurs and/or an object appears. This event and/or object are directly created by you, the observer. Before your observation, the event and/or object was simply a state of energy vibrating in an infinite domain of potential or possibilities. This includes trees, buildings, and cars, etc. It is your observation that causes the specific possibility to materialize. This effect has been shown experimentally for subatomic particles, atoms, and more recently for large molecules. Quantum mechanics tells us that although it may not be possible to do the same experiments for large objects such as people, since such objects are composed of atoms and molecules, the same conscious creation of these objects is what occurs in what we perceive with our five senses to be reality. In other words, ***you are constantly creating what you perceive.***

8.4.5 Uncertainty Principle

According to Nobel laureate Werner Heisenberg, small or microscopic objects such as electrons and atoms are not "real" in our everyday sense. They exist as "potentialities," and hence what we call the domain of "potentia," where there exist infinite possibilities and one of them is created by the **collapse of the wave function to a specific state or set of conditions**, as a consequence of our observation. Heisenberg proved mathematically that any observation disturbs things enough to prevent disproval of quantum mechanic's assertion that observation creates the property observed. Stated another way, the more accurately you know the exact position of a moving particle, say an electron, the less accurately you know its velocity, and conversely. This same principle applies to large objects, but the calculated uncertainties are so small as to be immeasurable. Because of this, we need

only use Newton's laws or Newtonian mechanics as opposed to quantum mechanics to track spaceships, satellites and planets. Newtonian mechanics is an approximation or simplified form of quantum mechanics.

8.4.6 Infinite Possibilities (Potentialities to Actuality)

What actually exists "out there" is an infinite number of "possibilities," in a domain that physicists refer to as the domain of "potentia." This infinite number of possibilities can be described by a complex mathematical expression called the quantum wave equation or quantum wave function, where you can think of the wave function as "spread out infinitely" over all of the possible outcomes. The probability of you perceiving a given outcome, namely, a certain event or the existence of a specific object under a given set of conditions, can be calculated from the square of the wave function. When you create a certain event by your observation, mathematically speaking, we say that you have caused the **wave function to collapse** from an infinite number of possibilities to a specific possibility or result.

World-renowned physicist and Nobel laureate, Eugene Wigner speculated that observation and instantaneous collapse of the wave function happens at the very last stage of the observation process, perhaps when awareness occurs. He also speculated that ***human conscious awareness*** might actually "reach out" in some unexplained manner and change the physical state of a system. All we know at this point in time is that somewhere on the scale between subatomic particles, atoms and large molecules, and that of big objects such as cars, buildings and human beings, there is a mysterious unexplained process wherein observation collapses the wave function to a specific possibility and observation. And it appears!

8.4.7 History Creation (Travelling Backwards in Time)

For decades, quantum mechanics predicted that your observation not only creates your present reality, but also creates the past history appropriate to that reality, i.e., you actually produce something backwards in time. Most scientists found this difficult to comprehend, much less believe. Quantum cosmologist John Archibald Wheeler suggested what he called a "delayed-choice experiment," which if carried out would determine whether or not one's observation actually could produce something backwards in time. For a long time, this was just conjecture, but in 1987, the experiment was performed and it confirmed that backwards-in-time history is created by the observer.

8.4.8 Duality (Wave and Particle)

Depending on how we measure the properties of an entity such as an electron, a neutron or a photon, they appear as both particles and waves. This attribute applies to big things such as human beings as well, although it is impossible to do the experiment for such large objects to prove this fact. This is the so-called duality of quantum mechanical measurement. As we will see in discussing this phenomenon, there are proven profound conclusions difficult to believe in our macroscopic world.

8.4.9 Multiple Places at Once (Probability of locating a particle)

If there is one electron, or photon, or neutron, or atom, or many other entities and two boxes in a given system, there is a calculable probability that the entity will be found in one of the boxes. Before you pick up either box to look inside, the entity is actually present in both boxes, and it is your looking that collapses the wave function and allows you to find it in one of the boxes. In fact, you can calculate from the square of the wave function the precise probability that you will find the entity in one of the boxes. The probability is directly related to the "waviness" of the wave equation. The "wavier" a set of conditions in the wave equation, the higher the probability of you finding a selected object in a chosen place.

8.4.10 Big is Like Small

Even though quantum mechanics is absolutely necessary to describe the state of being for small objects like electrons, neutrons, and photons, it applies to everything–you, me, the planet, the entire universe. In fact, cosmologists struggle with writing a wave equation for our universe. The reason is that the universe is made up of these same entities that obey the laws of quantum mechanics. It is just difficult to see the same profound effects when things get big. However, even with big things, we create our own reality.

8.4.11 Double-slit experiment with a single electron and Observer Effect

There is an even more subtle, but profound implication that follows from this electron's double-slit experiment, and it provides a glimpse of what lies at the very heart of the difference between classical physics and quantum physics. Consider the following. When a single electron is fired from the electron gun and travels towards the screen containing Slits A and B, through which slit does it pass in order to get to the photographic plate? Suppose it went through Slit A. In that case, Slit B would be unnecessary and we could just as well have closed it. But, with only Slit A open, the electron would not be most likely to arrive at the midpoint of the photographic plate exactly midway between Slits A and B as it does, but instead would end up at the point on the photographic plate exactly opposite Slit A. Since this is not the case, we can conclude that the electrons could not possibly have gone through Slit A. If we make the same argument for Slit B, we see that the single electron could not have gone through Slit B, either! What's happening here? The answer is that the single electron has gone through both slits at the same time! How could this possibly be? Does the electron interfere with itself as light waves do? Physicists decided to do the electron experiment again and this time to put a detector immediately on the other side of the two slits to see which slit the electron was actually going through. However, when they "peeked" by doing this, the experiment returned to the results observed when an electron acted as a particle and a pattern was seen only opposite each of the slits. No interference pattern formed. It was as if the electron "knew" that the experimenter was peeking, and it "decided" to go back to particle-like behaviour.

Our general sense of reality, conditioned by classical physics and our five senses says that this is nonsense, but it isn't. In quantum mechanics, we refer to this phenomenon as the superposition principle, and it makes perfect sense. It means that the state of motion of the electron has a probability of going through Slit A and a probability of going through Slit B, and the final result on the photographic plates is the sum, or in quantum mechanical language, the superposition of these probabilities. It is only by our observation that we "collapse" the wave function describing the system and the probability to a specific result. In essence, there are various probabilities before we observe the system; however, the very act of observing collapses the wave function to a specific possibility. In truth, our observation creates this reality.

In fact, the superposition principle demonstrates **three aspects of quantum mechanics** that appear to most of us to be in the realm of mysticism.

(i) The **first point** is that at our current state of human development and reality perception, it is impossible to form a clear picture in terms of our five senses about what is happening in the course of the physical process. We could not possibly visualize how an individual particle, such as an electron, a photon, or even an atom could simultaneously go through both slits.

(ii) The **second point** is the probabilistic nature of quantum mechanics, in that unlike the perfectly certain world of classical physics, it is no longer possible to predict what will happen when we make an observation, only the probability of what will occur. The deep philosophical and actual point here is that *classical physics is deterministic and quantum physics is probabilistic.* In classical physics, if I throw a ball up in the air, knowing all of the forces on the ball, and using Newton's laws, we can tell exactly where the ball will be at any point in time in the future; classical physics is deterministic. Not so in quantum physics. we can only tell the probability of finding the object at a given point at a given time.

(iii) The **third point** is that your observation actually creates your reality! To demonstrate this point, suppose we were to modify the double-slit experiment by putting a photographic plate detector immediately on the other side of Slit A and Slit B, so that we could determine which slit the electron passed through. What we find in this modification of the experiment is that sometimes the electron is detected near Slit A and sometimes it is detected near Slit B. It is impossible to predict which slit the electron will go through, but over a large number of electron firings from the electron gun, we find that the relative probabilities of going through each slit is 50-50. This illustrates that in quantum mechanics, predictions of the results of measurements are always statistical in character and not deterministic as in classical physics. After all, if we were firing a bullet through Slit A, we know that every single time we fire the gun at Slit A, the bullet will exit Slit A. Quantum mechanics deals in probabilities and not in certainties.

A final point concerning this modification of the experiment is the destruction of the interference pattern on the photographic plate. No longer do electrons tend to the midpoint of the photographic plate, but are split evenly between those arriving opposite Slits A and B. This demonstrates that whether we see particle-like or wave-like behaviour, depends on what we look for. **If we ask a particle-like question (which slit is the electron going through?), we get a particle-like answer. If we ask a wave-like question, (What is the final pattern of all of the accumulated electrons?), we get a wave-like answer.** In many respects, the double-split experiment embraces all of the mystery, the essence, and the power of quantum mechanics. In 1926, physicist, Max Born developed the quantitative interpretation of the probabilistic nature of quantum mechanics, for which he received the Nobel Prize 28 years later, in 1954.

8.4.12 Schrodinger's Cat and Wigner's Friend:

The superposition principle was of deep concern to Schrödinger, Einstein and other founding fathers of quantum mechanics. Schrödinger often said that had he known about this outcome, he would never have had anything to do with the development of quantum mechanics. He detested "these damned quantum jumps and probabilities!" He said this even after receiving the Nobel Prize in Physics. To elucidate his concern over the superposition principle, he created his famous Schrödinger cat thought experiment. In this "horrid" experiment, as he liked to call it, he envisioned a sealed box containing a cat, a glass flask of highly toxic hydrogen cyanide, a radioactive atom, uranium, for example, a Geiger counter, an electric relay and a hammer. When the atom of uranium decays, the Geiger counter detects the emitted radiation and sends a signal that activates the relay, releasing the hammer, smashing the flask, releasing the cyanide, , thereby killing the cat.

Radioactive decay is a quantum process, and therefore using Max Born's methodology, we can calculate the probability of the uranium atom decaying at any given time. Whether it has actually decayed at that instant and therefore, whether the cat is alive or dead, is not precisely known—we only know the probability of occurrence—at least until we peek into the box. According to quantum mechanics, the cat exists in two states of superposition—dead and alive—that is, it is both dead and alive at the same time until we look to find out. At that very moment, the wave equations for the dead and living cats collapse, and we know precisely whether the cat is alive or not. By looking, we create the final event. Schrödinger was trying to demonstrate the paradox of the superposition principle, which in nearly 70 years since modern quantum mechanics was first formulated, has never been found to be incorrect. Of course, to date, the theory has been applied to small entities such as electrons, photons, atoms and molecules, never to a living system.

The weirdness of the situation has now been amplified. If we are not able to communicate with our friend, what is happening to the cat and our friend? Did our friend look at the cat and found it dead, or did our friend look at the cat and found it alive, or incredibly, is it a combination of both scenarios at the same time? That strange combination of both scenarios would be suggested by the quantum wave function that has not collapsed. But now we have a conscious person involved, so how can his consciousness be in a state of both seeing the cat alive and seeing the cat dead? This is the Wigner's Friend problem.

In this case, in which the observation was carried out by someone else, the typical change in the wave function occurred only when some information (the yes or no of my friend) entered my consciousness. It follows that the quantum description of objects is influenced by impressions entering the consciousness.

8.4.13 Copenhagen Interpretation of Quantum Mechanics is based on three fundamental technical principles:

(i) **Probability**–The square of the wave function in a given region of space-time is the probability that the object will be found in that given region. It is important to note that this probability is not where the object is located, but where you will find it. What this means is that the object was not completely there until you observed it. If we consider the presence of a single atom in one of two boxes, quantum mechanics tells us that there is no atom in addition to its wave function. Each box contains the atom's wave function, and therefore, although we appear to be unable to fathom the fact, the atom itself is actually in both boxes until we observe the atom, at which time the wave function collapses and the atom is found in that single box. Indeed, the wave function is the only way to communicate information in quantum mechanics. In all actuality, the wave function is the entire story. Some physicists say that there is no atom in addition to the wave function, and actually the wave function is synonymous with the atom. But the atom is present as an entity of energy and information. The wave function certainly contains information, but not energy. The wave function does not carry specific information as to how a particular entity will behave or a specific event will occur. Rather, it is an expression of potential or statistical probability. This is in stark contrast to classical physics where answers are always exact and specific and the future of a given system is precisely predictable.

(ii) **Uncertainty**–As discussed above, according to Heisenberg's Uncertainty Principle, if we consider the position and momentum (mass x velocity) of a small particle such as an atom, the more precisely we know about its velocity or momentum, the less precisely we can know its position. The fact is that any observation disturbs things enough to prevent disproval of quantum mechanic's assertion that observation creates the property observed.

(iii) **Complementarity between particle- and wave-pictures:** The particle-like and wave-like behaviours of a microscopic object are "complementary." A complete description of the object requires that we make use of both behaviours, but never at the same time. This is a statement of the complementarity of Newtonian or classical mechanics and quantum mechanics. The macro world obeys Newtonian mechanics and the micro or quantum world obeys quantum mechanics. If we do a wave-like experiment, we will always get a wave-like answer; if we do a particle-like experiment, we will always get a particle-like answer.

8.5 Introducing the Role of Ganesha Consciousness

As we have seen from the above discussion that the 'Observer Effect' or the consciousness has got an inescapable and a significant role in the measurement process.

Manifest matter is preceded by quantum possibilities or potentialities. There are two realms of reality—potentiality and actuality. Conscious choice collapses the possibilities into manifest actuality. Since this choice is made from a state of consciousness beyond the ego, we refer to it as a "higher" or "quantum" consciousness, spiritual traditions refer to it as God. And since our conscious choices are shaped by higher consciousness this process can be described by the term downward causation.

Conscious choice precipitates the collapse of quantum possibilities (waves) of each world into the manifest realm (of actualities). The multiple parallel worlds do not directly interact; consciousness mediates their interaction. The collapse is nonlocal, meaning that it requires no local communication or exchange of signals. The need for local communication via signals holds true only for space-time; quantum consciousness is nonlocal and therefore outside of space and time.

The quantum collapse from possibility to actuality is discontinuous. The word transcendent, which we apply to the realm of pure potentiality, evokes both nonlocality and discontinuity.

In the transcendent quantum realm of pure potentiality, consciousness remains undivided from its possibilities and there is no experience. Collapse produces "dependent co-arising" of an experiencing subject and an object that is experienced.

Creativity is fundamentally a phenomenon of consciousness discontinuously manifesting truly the new possibilities from transcendent potentiality. This is why, in ancient traditions, creativity was referred to as a marriage between (transcendent) heaven and (immanent) earth. The mind gives meaning to the interaction of consciousness and matter. The value of creative work comes from what we intuit, what Plato called archetypes. The role of the brain is to make representations of mental meaning.

Creativity is invention or discovery of new meaning. What is truly new is meaning invented or discovered using old or new archetypal contexts and combinations thereof.

8.5.1 The Case Against Materialism

The case against pure materialism, and against the claim that consciousness must be derived from matter, is actually very strong. In the first place, there is no actual scientific evidence that consciousness arises from matter. All we have is evidence that the content of consciousness is linked in some way to the functioning of the physical brain, but that hardly amounts to concrete scientific evidence that the material brain must be the source of consciousness. A link between two things does not necessarily imply that one created the other.

Now we have yet another strong reason to doubt this dogmatic claim that consciousness must be derived from matter, and that comes from the very formulation of quantum mechanics. Right from the onset we can see that quantum mechanics pivots around the observer. The formulation provides rules for what the conscious observer finds and not rules for the behaviour of matter directly.

A direct experiential interpretation of quantum mechanics, without adhoc additions, inserted by hand, tells us that, in fact, particles are dependently originated. Crucially, this dependent arising of the object requires the act of measurement or observation by the conscious observer. Using Heisenberg's terminology, we can say that physical particles only make the transition from the 'possible' to the 'actual' upon the act of measurement by the observer. How then can the reverse also be possible? In other words, how then can physical particles also be considered to be the cause of the mind of the observer?

In other words, mind and consciousness cannot be derived from matter. It is quantum mechanics that tells us that this is impossible, since there is no inherently existing elementary particle that is not dependently arisen. And given that one of the factors required for its dependent arising as an actual particle is the mind that apprehends it, how can this entity, or collection of such entities, be what the mind is purely derived from, in the first place? That would be totally illogical.

As mentioned, quantum mechanics does not directly provide rules for the behaviour of particles per se. Quantum mechanics, instead, only provides rules for the results of measurements by the observer. So, all these persistent attempts at trying to get rid of the conscious observer, from quantum mechanics, may be destined to fail, simply because the observer is an intrinsic part of the quantum mechanics formulation. There is no point in denying this fact just to cling on to materialism. In other words, quantum mechanics is directly pointing to the fact that materialism is probably an incorrect idea.

8.5.2 More on Observer, Consciousness and its characteristics

As we have seen earlier that the 'observer effect' leads to the conclusion that the observer's looking must involve some interaction involving nonmatter because material interactions can only convert possibility waves into other possibility waves, never actualities. This nanmatter is ***observer's consciousness.***

But **what is consciousness?** According to Quantum Physics, the Consciousness has the following definitions/characteristics:

(i) Consciousness is the ground of all being; matter consists of possibilities of consciousness itself. Since the consciousness is choosing from itself, this assertion avoids the paradox of dualism. How does consciousness interact with matter without a signal? Quantum physics gives the answer: there is no signal. The signal-less communication is called ***nonlocality.***

Physicists speak of "locality" and "nonlocality". A locus is a place: it has a particular relationship to space; and a location can change with time. Cause and effect, too, are related to time and space: a cue ball, which is here, "now" strikes a billiard ball, which is there, "then" deflecting it into a side pocket. The cue ball is said to be the cause of an effect on the billiard ball: a "local" event has transpired. The best way in which to translate "nonlocality" is to say that events in this category are not confined to a relationship in time or space. Put another way, nonlocality is transcendent of locality, similar to the way that the omnipotent would have to be transcendent of cause-and effect.

Physicist David Bohm, as a consequence of his quantum research, began to sense a nonlocal reality at the base of our physical universe. A development in physics had made it clear that an observer (experimenter) cannot be considered to be objectively isolated from the observed (experiment): in other words, an experiment is not unaffected by the experimenter. Indeed, physics had gone so far as to conclude, as a result of laboratory experiments, that the outcome of an experiment can depend upon the intent of the observer's investigation. If the cause (physicist's intent) cannot be conclusively separated from the effect (experimental outcome), what are the broader implications for assumptions based on "locality"?

In 1959, David Bohm initiated a series of dialogues between him and J. Krishnamurti (such as that published as "The Ending of Time"). By 1974, Bohm had co-authored a paper entitled "On the Intuitive Understanding of Nonlocality as Implied by Quantum Theory". "Parts", said the theoretical physicist, "are seen to be in immediate connection...extending ultimately and in principle to the entire universe. Thus, one is led to a new notion of unbroken wholeness which denies the classical idea of analysability of the world into separately and independently-existent parts..."

Bohm's earlier writings along these lines inspired another physicist, John Bell, the author of Bell's Theorem. Bell initially set out to disprove the principle of nonlocality, but his mathematical conclusions actually supported Bohm's premise. The mechanics of the calculations in Bell's Theorem lent themselves to laboratory experiments—most notably one in 1982 performed by physicists in Paris.

Bell's Theorem states, in effect, that after two [subatomic] particles interact in a conventional way, then move apart outside the range of the interaction, the particles continue to influence each other instantaneously via a real connection, which joins them together with undiminished strength no matter how far apart they may roam.…Bell's Theorem says not merely that superluminal connections are possible, but that they are necessary to make our kind of universe work.…Bell's Theorem shows that…things are hooked together by an invisible, underlying network of superluminal connections." Bell's Theorem tells us that there is no such thing as 'separate parts'. All of the 'parts' of the universe are connected in an intimate and immediate way… 'Common-sense' ideas are inadequate even to describe macroscopic events—events of the everyday world!" (e.g., cause and effect)

Suppose that you simultaneously fired off, in different directions, "paired" photons. By paired, we mean that one of them, say, was negatively charged, while its twin was positively charged. Let us say that, mid-flight, the polarity of one of the photons was mechanically switched. This change should not affect the other photon, causally, since both are racing away in entirely different directions. And, yet, the remaining photon will simultaneously react to the identity switch of its twin—by instantly reversing its own polarity. Such a supernatural occurrence as that demonstrated to be physical actuality, can have only one reasonable explanation, in terms of "locality" or normal causality: somehow the first photon communicated its change of state to the second photon.

However, in our known portion of the universe, anything which moves (or is transmissible)—within the confines of relative time and space—is limited to an upward speed. Not anything, in the natural world, can be "propagated" at faster than the speed of light, according to a fundament of physics. Therefore, any earthly message which is transmitted between subatomic particles could be communicated, over a distance, at no more than 186,000 miles per second. This experiment was repeated, this time outside of a laboratory. Given the minuscule size of a subatomic particle, any interactions over a mile or so apart are akin to "universal" distances. The experiment was conducted by a physics team at the University of Geneva, who effected the phenomenon at a distance of approximately seven miles. "Measurements at the two sites", says the Encyclopedia Britannica Online (Year in Review: 1997), "showed that each photon 'knew' its partner's state in less time than a signal traveling at light speed could have conveyed the information—a vindication of the [nonlocality] theory of quantum mechanics (but a problem, for some, for theories of causation)."

Such powerful information is co-opted by the military. Physicists in government research facilities, of the major powers, are siphoning this research into a system for the transmission of codes (negative and positive photons can represent the zeros and ones of binary encoding, and changes in their polarity can signal a message). But there is an even more critical reason why such information will be overlooked or dismissed, even though it can no longer be categorized as mere conjecture. If there is indeed a supernatural force or intelligence, it is not unreasonable to suppose that it forms "an immediate connection" between every particle (and antiparticle) throughout the realm of space and time, "nonlocally": "extending", as Bohm put it, "ultimately and in principle to the entire universe". It would connect the observer (me) and the observed (you) in an "unbroken wholeness which denies the classical idea...of...separately and independently-existent parts". Do we live that way, with a recognition and acknowledgement— unequivocally—that this is the actual, physical condition of our biosphere ? Or do we ignore this truth, even when it is proven?

(ii) There is no mathematics for collapse of the wave function; no continuous algorithm can be given for it; collapse is discontinuous. What is discontinuity? As discussed earlier, when an electron jumps from one atomic orbit to another, it does so without going through intermediate space, This electron's quantum leap (or quantum jump) is an example discontinuity.

(iii) Quantum measurement in the brain is **tangled hierarchical,** meaning that there is a circular relationship among the components of the brain. This gives self-reference. In the process of quantum measurement involving the tangled-hierarchical brain, consciousness splits itself into a subject (that experiences) and an object (that is experienced). In this process (that the consciousness is nothing but the awareness of its own awareness, that is, Ganesha awareness), it identifies with the brain.

8.5.3 The Nature of the Quantum Wave Function

The Delayed Choice Quantum Eraser and Quantum Entanglement

An innovative experimental set-up for the double-slit experiment, that is particularly appropriate for exploring the nature of the *quantum wave function*, is an intriguing version of the experiment known as the delayed choice quantum eraser.

Recall that, in the basic double-slit experiment, a particle like a photon would pass through both slits if no measurement is made to ascertain which slit the particle went through. This is because, without a measurement being made, the *quantum wave function* would not collapse, and the particle actually does not manifest as a single particle at a single position. The quantum wave function would continue un-collapsed and represent merely a probability distribution of possible measurement findings *if and only if* we make an actual measurement. Effectively, we can say that the particle is behaving like a wave and passing through both slits simultaneously, and would form an interference pattern on the screen, as a wave would do.

It is only the act of measurement—to ascertain which slit the particle passes through—that would cause the *collapse of the wave function* and force the particle to manifest at one or other slit. If the particle did that, there would then not be an interference pattern on the screen.

Now suppose we do the measurement of which slit the particle passes through in an unusual and indirect way. First, we can delay the choice of whether or not we make an actual measurement—that tells us which slit the particle passes through—until *after* the original particle actually hits the screen. This can actually be done, and is what the phrase "delayed choice" refers to.

We can also do something even more unusual. Not only can we delay the choice of whether or not we actually make the measurement till after the original particle hits the screen, we can also delay the "choice" of whether or not the experimental set-up provides us, the observers, with the actual information of which slit the particle passed through. And this choice can also be made after the original particle has already hit the screen. This is the so-called "quantum eraser" part of the experiment, since the experimental set-up can act as though the "which-slit" information has been erased and cannot reach the observer.

The "delayed choice" and the "quantum eraser" aspects of the experiment can be achieved through the use of *quantum entanglement*; in this case, through the use of entangled pairs of photons. Entangled photons have properties that are correlated in such a way that the *quantum wave function* of each of the photons cannot be described independently of each other. Essentially, they become one system. Because of this, a measurement of certain properties of one photon would provide information about the other photon.

In the delayed choice quantum eraser experiment, one of the photons in an entangled pair is called the *signal photon* and the other is called the *idler photon*. The basic strategy is to allow the signal photon to travel to the screen while directing its corresponding idler photon onto a different path. Then, only after the signal photon has already hit the screen, do we make a measurement on its corresponding idler photon in order to determine which slit the signal photon emerged from. That is how the *delayed choice* aspect of the experiment can be implemented.

We can also arrange the experimental set-up such that some of the idler photons would encounter devices designed to "scramble" the information that it carries concerning which slit its corresponding signal photon emerged from. After this information has been scrambled, the observer can no longer obtain the "which slit" information from measurements made on the idler photon. This is the *quantum eraser* part of the experiment.

This delayed choice quantum eraser experiment also illustrates the peculiar quality of *quantum entanglement*, whereby the measurement of one of the entangled pair of photons actually appears to affect the other photon, as though a "message" has been sent between them, a "message" that is faster than the speed of light. In other words, the measurement made on one of the entangled pair of photons—in this case, the idler photon—appears to result in a "message" from the idler photon telling the signal photon that it has to now "decide" which slit it had passed through.

Here, the apparent "message" being sent to the signal photon, by having a measurement made on the idler photon, is even more dramatic than being faster than the speed of light. The "message" appears to have been sent **backwards in time**! This is because we have already allowed the signal photon to hit the screen before a measurement is made on the idler photon. That, in the first place, is why it is called a "delayed choice" experiment.

The measurement made on the idler photons, nonetheless, still appears to affect the pattern the signal photons leave on the screen, even though the measurement on each idler photon was made, every time, *after* the corresponding signal photon had already hit the screen. So, if we consider that a message has been sent by the idler photon to its corresponding signal photon, it could only have been sent backwards in time!

8.5.4 The Two "Weird" Things About the Double-Slit Experiment

A simple way to obtain an overview of the delayed choice quantum eraser version of the double-slit experiment is to look at the two "weird" things that would arise *if we were thinking along the lines of a mind-matter duality*— i.e., where the object (the photon) is distinct from the mind (the observer).

It is important to realize that there are actually *two* things that are "weird" about this experiment. One weird thing is that, although the photon displays the properties of a wave (like producing an interference pattern), we only see a photon as a particle whenever we make an actual observation. This, as we know, is the *collapse of the wave function*. To reiterate, before the observation, the *quantum wave function* provides us with a probability distribution of where the photon may be found *if and only if* we make an actual observation. When we actually make an observation, however, the photon is only found in one place. This is one of the *two* weird things about the double-slit experiment.

The second weird thing is this: If we now place a detector so that we can tell which slit the photon went through, the interference pattern disappears. It is as though, having a detector there, forces the photon to choose which slit it goes through. Now here's the real peculiarity concerning this: we do not actually have to make an observation for the interference pattern to disappear. Just having the detector there will cause the interference pattern to vanish. It is as though the photon knows that we can spy on it if we want to, and that is enough for it to stop performing the "interference pattern trick." All that is required is an experimental set-up that enables the observer to make an observation *if* he wants to, and the interference pattern disappears. No actual observation at the slits is required. Also, if we remove the detector at the slits, the interference pattern reappears. So, it is the experimental set-up that determines the result.

To make this phenomenon even more intriguing, we have the *delayed choice quantum eraser* experiment, whereby the information on which slit the photon went through can only be obtained *after* the photon hits the screen (this is possible through the use of *quantum entanglement*). This does not seem to make any difference to the result, i.e., as long as there is the ability to tell which slit the photon went through, no interference pattern occurs. It is as though the photon realizes that we can determine which slit it went through after it hits the screen, and that is already enough to stop it from performing the interference-pattern trick.

To make things still more intriguing, if we now insert another device (this is the eraser part) so that it now obscures the information concerning which slit the photon went through, the interference pattern reappears. Now, it is as though the photon has found out that the information from our detector (that allows us to see which slit it went through) is now being scrambled by another device so that we can no longer obtain this information. That being the case, the photon is now happy to perform its interference-pattern trick again.

So, what actually is going on? It almost appears like the photons know what we are able to do in terms of spying on them, and that these photons are conspiring to thwart us in our quest to determine how they are performing their tricks! Of course, no one actually thinks that the photons are sentient beings involved in an elaborate conspiracy to trick us, but that really appears to be what is happening. This is the second weird thing about the double-slit experiment.

All this sounds extremely strange, and that has, in fact, been the central mystery of quantum mechanics for over a century now. However, remember that, here, we have considered the findings of the double-slit experiment *in terms of a mind-matter duality*. It is actually this mind-matter duality that led to these two so-called "weird" effects in the double-slit experiment.

Let us now, instead, consider the findings of the delayed choice quantum eraser version of the double-slit experiment in terms of a *direct experiential interpretation of quantum mechanics*.

8.5.5 The Nature of the Quantum Wave Function

Keep in mind that there are two key effects about the double-slit experiment that involve the observer:

1. The *collapse of the wave function* upon measurement by an observer.

2. Changes in the probability distribution of the measurement results that depend on whether or not the "which slit" information can reach an observer.

Both these effects point to an observer effect in quantum physics. This means that any claim to a solution that negates the observer effect must account for *both* these effects.

The second effect, though, does not require an observer to be physically present and actually noting the results *at the time* of the experiment. What this tells us is this. If the experimental conditions enable us to tell which slit the signal photon passed through (if we wanted to find out), no interference pattern would emerge on the screen. If the experimental conditions were such that we cannot tell which slit the signal photon passed through (even if we wanted to find out), then an interference pattern would emerge on the screen.

The key factor is whether or not the "which slit" information is available to the conscious observer. If the information is available, no interference pattern forms. If the information is not available, an interference pattern forms.

This result provides us with very important information concerning the nature of the *quantum wave function*. What it means is that the probability distribution for the measurement results changes upon altering the experimental conditions, even when the experiment is conducted without any conscious observer being present to note the results directly at that time. In other words, we can alter the *quantum wave function* just by altering the experimental set-up.

Note, however, that this does *not* mean that the *collapse of the wave function* can occur without the observer actually reading the results. All that has happened, without the observer present, is that the probability distribution of possible results has changed. No *collapse of the wave function* has occurred in this process.

In other words, while we know that there is a change in the probability distribution of the possible results—concerning where the set of photons end up on the screen—we still do not know where any *one* particular photon ends up. We still only have a probability distribution of possible results, and not the actual results, if the observer does not make an actual observation of the results. In other words, the *quantum wave function* has changed but it has still not collapsed.

So, what does this tell us about the *quantum wave function*? It tells us that the crucial factor in determining the form of the *quantum wave function* are the possible *experiential events* that the experimental set-up would allow the observer to have. In other words, the set of possible *experiential events* determine the *quantum wave function*. If we change the set of possible *experiential events* by changing the experimental set-up, the *quantum wave function* would change accordingly to reflect this new set of possible *experiential events* that the observer could encounter.

Note that this mechanism is akin to a change in the *preferred basis* depending on what the observer chooses to measure. In other words, a change in the possible set of *experiential events*—which, of course, would change when a different property is being measured—would lead to the *quantum wave function* being altered to reflect this change in the set of possible *experiential events*.

All this means that it is the *experiential events*—that are the acts of observation involving both the particle and the conscious observer—that are the primary reality that the *quantum wave function* provides information on. A change in the possible set of *experiential events* changes the *quantum wave function*, even without an observer being present at the time. Nonetheless, an actual act of measurement by a conscious observer is still required for the *collapse of the wave function*.

A *direct experiential interpretation of quantum mechanics* thus explains the two so-called "weird" effects of the double-slit experiment. These effects are actually only weird in terms of a mind-matter duality. If we adopt a middle way approach—as provided by Madhyamika philosophy—without positing a mind-matter dichotomy, and consider instead that the *experiential events* are the *primary reality* that quantum mechanics deals with, we can arrive at a consistent interpretation of the double-slit experiment that is free of contradictions.

Note that if we consider the *experiential events* to be the primary reality, rather than the particles (in this case, the photons) themselves, it also explains the peculiar property of a "message" being sent faster than the speed of light—or in this case, even backwards in time—in cases involving *quantum entanglement.* In other words, this idea of a message being sent, between an entangled pair of particles, only arises *if* we consider the particles to be inherently existing entities, that are independent of the conscious observer, in the first place.

Now, if it is the *experiential events* that actually constitute our reality, we do not need to posit a "message" being sent between the idler photon and its corresponding signal photon. What we need to realize is that a measurement made on the idler photon changes the set of possible *experiential events* in the experimental set-up, and this changes the *quantum wave function* accordingly. As already mentioned, this process is akin to a change in the *preferred basis* upon changing the *observable* we choose to measure.

Thus, a *direct experiential interpretation of quantum mechanics* not only explains the two so-called "weird" effects of the double-slit experiment, it also explains why, in cases of *quantum entanglement*, apparent "messages" can be sent faster than the speed of light, or in our case, even backwards in time.

All these "weird" effects appear only because we have been inappropriately trying to fit the formulation of quantum mechanics into a philosophical framework that posits a mind-matter dichotomy. The problem of messages travelling faster than the speed of light, or even backwards in time, arises only *if* we insist on forcing quantum mechanics into a framework of materialism, and trying to negate the critical role of consciousness in science and reality.

To conclude, in a *direct experiential interpretation of quantum mechanics*, we accept that the mathematical formulation actually represents our reality, without resorting to all sorts of additional hypothetical *ad hoc* conditions, inserted arbitrarily, just so that we can fit the formulation of quantum mechanics into some preconceived and biased notion of what our reality should be like. All such attempts, over the last century, to fit quantum mechanics into a predetermined view of reality, have, in fact, run into serious conceptual difficulties.

The preconceived notion, of what many scientists think our reality should be like, is this notion of a mind-matter dichotomy. And since most scientists choose to resolve this dichotomy by adopting the stance of materialism, the preconceived notion of reality that physicists have persistently tried to force the formulation of quantum mechanics to fit into, is the idea of materialism—particularly the notion that consciousness must, somehow or other, be derived purely from matter.

It is crucial to realize, however, that these philosophical ideas are *not at all* suggested by the formulation of quantum mechanics. Quantum mechanics does *not* provide any indication of a mind-matter duality, and certainly does *not* suggest, in even the slightest way, that consciousness is derived from matter. Quantum mechanics actually suggests the reverse: that both the idea of a mind-matter duality, and the assumption that consciousness is derived from matter, are, in fact, incorrect.

CHAPTER 9

QUANTUM ENTANGLEMENT AND CONNECTION WITH GANESHA CONSCIOUSNESS

Hiddenly

To each other linked are,

That thou canst not stir a flower

Without troubling of a star.

– Radin, Dean

9.1 Introduction to Quantum Entanglement

Small particles such as electrons, atoms and molecules– the building blocks of all material things– experience a mysterious effect called "quantum entanglement," wherein a change in one particle instantaneously affects another particle at a significant distance, even though there appears to be no force field between the two particles. For example, it is possible to have two electrons, proximate to each other that are paired together, one spinning to the left, and the other spinning to the right. If these electrons are now separated by hundreds of kilometres, and then the spin on one electron is reversed, the other electron instantly reverses its spin as well, as if it "knew" when and what to do!1 This communication between these two electrons takes place instantaneously and superluminally, that is, immeasurably beyond the speed of light. All experiments to-date suggest that this same effect would occur if these electrons were galaxies apart, separated by millions of light-years. The communication would still be instantaneous and immeasurably faster than the speed of light. How this communication occurs is still a mystery to scientists, as no apparent forces are involved.

Quantum entanglement is a physical phenomenon that occurs when pairs or groups of particles are generated such that the quantum state of each particle cannot be described independently of the state of the others, even when the particles are separated by a large distance. Measurements of physical properties such as position, momentum, spin, and polarization, performed on entangled particles are found to be correlated. For example, if a pair of particles is generated in such a way that their total spin is known to be zero, and one particle is found to have clockwise spin on a certain axis, the spin of the other particle, measured on the same axis, will be found to be counterclockwise, as is to be expected due to their entanglement. However, this behaviour gives rise to seemingly paradoxical effects: any measurement of a particle's properties results in an irreversible wave function collapse of that particle and changes the original quantum state. With entangled particles, such measurements affect the entangled system as a whole.

Such phenomena were the subject of a 1935 paper by Albert **Einstein**, Boris **Podolsky**, and Nathan **Rosen**

(EPR, in short) , and several papers by Erwin Schrödinger shortly thereafter, describing what came to be known as the **EPR** paradox. Einstein and others considered such behaviour to be impossible, as it violated the local realism view of causality (Einstein referring to it as "spooky action at a distance"). EPR asserted that if such an instant entanglement phenomenon is accepted between the two particles separated by a very large distance; this will violate the maximum limit of the speed of light. Therefore, they argued that the accepted formulation of quantum mechanics must therefore be incomplete. Only after the realization of an experiment suggested by Bell, was the nonlocal nature of quantum mechanics widely accepted.

A quantumly entangled system is defined to be one whose quantum state cannot be factored as a product of states of its local constituents; that is to say, they are not individual particles but are an inseparable whole. In entanglement, one constituent cannot be fully described without considering the other(s). The state of a composite system is always expressible as a sum, or superposition, of products of states of local constituents; it is entangled if this sum cannot be written as a single product term.

9.1.1 What is Nonlocality in Quantum Entanglement?

A non-local connection links up one location with another without crossing space, without decay, and without delay.

These connections have three identifying characteristics:

(i) They are unmediated (no connecting signal is involved, that means it is a signal-less communication),

(ii) unmitigated (the strength of the correlations does not fade with increasing distance), and

(iii) immediate (they are instantaneous).

Basically, the general "principle of locality" requires that "for an action at one point to have an influence at another point, something in the space between the points, such as a field, must mediate the action". In view of the theory of relativity, the speed at which such an action, interaction, or influence can be transmitted between distant points in space cannot exceed the speed of light. This formulation is also known as "Einstein locality" or "local relativistic causality". It is often stated as "nothing can propagate faster than light, be it energy or merely information" or simply "no spooky action-at-a-distance", as Einstein himself put it.

The phenomenon of entanglement between quantum systems raised the nonlocality problem first noted in the EPR paper:

"A projective measurement on a quantum system at one space location instantly collapses the state of an entangled counterpart at a distant location."

Quantum mechanical nonlocality refers to this apparent entanglement-mediated violation of Einstein locality. Although entanglement correlations are affected instantaneously, they cannot be harnessed for faster-than-light communications. The reason is that the outcome of the local projective measurement is itself statistic and cannot be predicted beforehand.

The three physical aspects of "non-locality" and therefore entanglement are: **First,** interaction is instantaneous, i.e., faster than the speed of light. **Second,** because there is no field or medium necessary for this contact to be made or maintained, nothing can block it from occurring. And **third,** distance does not weaken the contact or interaction. It could just as well occur over the distance of many galaxies as over several meters, both with the same intensity of interaction, and the same time required to occur.

Entanglement is a metaphysical-like aspect of quantum mechanics. In simple terms, entanglement maintains that observation of one object can instantaneously influence the behaviour of another object, even at very great distances, and even when there appears to be no physical force existing between the two objects. *Entanglement is a prime example of the non-local nature of quantum mechanics and is an integral part of the concept of "connectedness" in the universe.* In principle, any two objects that have ever interacted, are forever entangled– the behaviour of one instantaneously influences the other. The meta-physicist would say, "We are all connected in some manner," and in doing so, refer to Individual Consciousness and Universal Consciousness, both being integrally one. *This is, what is called, Non-duality or*

Advaita, or in other words: merging of Individual Consciousness with the Ganesha Consciousness into one indistinguishable state.

Nonlocality is subdivided by some physicists into three types. Type-I is spatial nonlocality; type-II is temporal nonlocality; and type-III nonlocality is both spatial and temporal.

9.1.2 What is 'Spatial Nonlocality' in Quantum Entanglement?

Until recently, the two (or more) quantumly entangled objects, satisfying the criterion of non-locality, could be located at any distance apart. This is called the 'Spatial Nonlocality' in Quantum Entanglement. It is to this type of large separation to which Einstein referred to as 'spooky action' because it violated the maximum limit of speed of light.

9.1.3 What is 'Temporal Nonlocality' in Quantum Entanglement?

The non-locality of quantum mechanics, as manifested by entanglement, does not apply only to particles with space-like separation, but also to particles with time-like separation. If the two objects are located at two different times (instead of different points in space) and are entangled, this is called 'temporal nonlocality'. It means that the second object (which was generated at a subsequent time) was entangled with the first object which existed in the past, and vice versa. ***The future,***

past, present, and consciousness are entangled within the quantum continuum.

9.2 Perception of Time and Nonlocality

Time is a concept that spans the human condition. Psychological research shows that just about all of human experience is dependent upon and influenced by how individuals perceive time, localize themselves consciously within space and time and process their temporally-based perceptions and experiences. Classical physics has successfully allowed us to calculate and measure time at the macroscale while relativistic physics demonstrates how time and space are conjugate pairs that manifest in a unified continuum. With the establishment of quantum mechanics, concepts such as entanglement and nonlocality allow us to construct a new cosmological model of time that connects with cognitive perception— one that asserts that time is perceived in a complementary timeful and timeless state. In the timeful state, the mind perceives time in its localized, linear, and causal aspects; while in its timeless state as non-local, symmetrical, and entangled.

Many of the spiritual traditions throughout history maintain a similar position of human consciousness as having the capacity to abide within these complementary modes of existence. How time, and conceptions about the past, present or future are therefore illusions, as there is no 'future' or 'past'. However, when considered from the perspective of quantum mechanics, timespace is a continuum, a unity, and time does not exist independent of this continuum, except as an act of perceptual registration by consciousness or mechanical means.

The recognition of the mind's ability to experience both the localized and non-localized complementary aspects of time was the impetus for the ancient Indian mystics to develop advanced mental techniques to master time within the domain of human consciousness. The goal of these disciplines was to liberate from the inherent cognitive filters that limit one's consciousness into the distorted and fragmented perception of time.

The mechanism that reduces human consciousness into experiencing time in its temporally localized state is what is referred to as veiled non-locality. The term implies how consciousness disguises its wholeness and nonlocality in order to produce local processes. This filtering process allows for specific observations and thoughts in a classical world of everyday experience, while keeping quantum and general relativistic processes out of sight.

9.3 Time is Entangled

Time cannot be separate from the continuum except when perceived as such by an observing consciousness or measuring device, thereby inducing a collapse of the wave function of time; experienced as the present, past, or future. Time, be it considered a dimension known as timespace, or as a perceived aspect of the quantum continuum, is also subject to entanglement, as all aspects of time are interconnected and indistinguishable until perceived thereby inducing a collapse of the wave function. "A" future can therefore effect "a" past and change it through entanglement and by influencing the wave function.

The quantum continuum is without dimensions and encompasses space and time in its basic unity of oneness. Everything within the quantum continuum can be influenced by the local effect and distant effects simultaneously at and beyond light speeds. Therefore, the future, and the "present" being part of this continuum can influence the past by effecting the wave function of the past, present, future, and thus, the space-time continuum, as all are entangled. Time-space is interactional, and can contract to near nothingness and then continue to contract in a negative direction such that the time traveler can journey into the past.

9.4 Learning from Scriptures about Quantum Entanglement

Thus, the learning of the ancient Hindu scriptures and Quantum Entanglement can be summarized into the following three key points:

(i) There exists a transcendental, infinite, non-local, dimensionless, unchanging reality that is obscured from the limited cognitive perception of the human senses;

(ii) This foundational reality is veiled by means of a cognitive illusion that limits the consciousness into a localized, linear, and dimensionally finite perception of time.

(iii) Advanced mental training needs to be developed and practiced in order to liberate one's consciousness from the illusory cognitive limitations of the mind via a perceptual reframing of time into its fundamental non-local, entangled state.

9.5 Scaling up of Entanglement from Microscopic to Macroscopic Level

Scientists are now finding that there are ways in which the effects of microscopic entanglements "scale up" into our macroscopic world. Entangled connections between carefully prepared atomic-sized objects can persist over many miles. There are theoretical descriptions showing how tasks can be accomplished by entangled groups without the members of the group communicating with each other in any conventional way. Some scientists suggest that the remarkable degree of coherence displayed in living systems might depend in some fundamental way on quantum effects like entanglement. Others suggest that conscious awareness is caused or related in some important way to entangled particles in the brain. Some even propose that the ***entire universe is a single, self-entangled object.*** If these speculations are correct, then what would human experience be like in such an interconnected universe? Would we occasionally have strange feelings of connectedness with loved ones, even at a distance? Would such experiences evoke a feeling of awe that there's more to reality than common sense implies? Could "entangled minds" be involved when you hear the telephone ring and somehow know—instantly—who's calling? If we did have such experiences, could they be due to real information that somehow bypassed the usual sensory channels? Or are such reports better understood as coincidences or delusions?

The idea of the universe as an interconnected whole is not new; for millennia it's been one of the core assumptions underlying Eastern philosophies. What is new is that Western science is slowly beginning to realize that some elements of that ancient lore might have been correct. Of course, adopting a new ontology is not to be taken lightly.

Cosmologists have learned that we might have accidentally overlooked 96% of the universe. The missing majority of the universe has been dubbed "dark" energy and matter. We know next to nothing about it, and it's spawning whole new concepts about the structure and evolution of the universe. As theories of cosmology are being reconsidered, new light is dawning on astronomical anomalies first observed decades ago.

Molecular biologists, who till recently regarded large segments of the genome as "junk DNA" because no one knew what it was good for, have been astonished to find strong commonalities among DNA base-pairs in humans, chickens, dogs, and fish. It appears that some aspects of DNA have been ultra-conserved for hundreds of millions of years, and that previous assumptions about what is important in DNA were wrong. For a century, neuroscientists believed that neurons in the brain do not regenerate, that once there is a brain injury or as neurons die in the course of aging, normal mental functioning inevitably deteriorates. Now we've learned that the dogma was wrong—**brain neurons do regenerate.** The plasticity of the brain is much greater than previously expected. This helps shed new light on previous observations that were ignored because they didn't make any sense. In a case study reported in 1980 in the journal 'Science', during a routine examination for a minor medical ailment, a student at Sheffield University in Great Britain was found to have virtually no brain. But that didn't stop him from enjoying an IQ of 126 and graduating with first-class honours in mathematics.

Physicists have been able to entangle ensembles of trillions of atoms in gaseous form, and entanglement has been demonstrated among the atoms of relatively large chunks (centimeter square) of salt. Entangled photons shot through sheets of metal have been shown to remain entangled after punching through to the other side. Photons also remain entangled after being sent through 50 kilometers of optical fiber, and while being transmitted through the open atmosphere. Clusters of four entangled photons have been demonstrated to make quantum computing significantly easier to accomplish than it was previously imagined. And organic molecules, like tetraphenylporphyrin (C44H30N4), have been successfully entangled.

Physicists have even speculated that entanglement extends to everything in the universe, because as far as we know, **all energy and all matter emerged out of a single, primordial Big Bang.** And thus, everything came out of the chute already entangled. Some further speculate that empty space, the quantum vacuum itself, may be filled with entangled particles. Such proposals suggest that despite everyday appearances, we might be living within a holistic, deeply interconnected reality. To be clear, these speculations are being proposed by traditional physicists, not by starry-eyed new agers or mystics.

9.6 Evidence of Quantumly Entangled Twins: A True Story

Identical twins who grew up separately provide a rare opportunity to study how environment versus heredity influences human development.

Four weeks later, at the now-defunct Knoop Children's Home in Troy, Ohio, the brothers became separated when one of them was adopted by Ernest Springer, a utility-company lineman, and his wife, Sarah, who brought him to their home in Piqua.

The Springers would likely have adopted both boys. But, for reasons still unclear, they were told the other twin had died during birth. In fact, however, the second boy was adopted two weeks later by Jess Lewis, a Lima public-school boilerman, and his wife, Lucille.

When the Lewises completed their adoption papers, one Miami County probate-court official gasped: "That's what [the Springers] named their son, too!"

Jim Springer was in his teens when he was told that his twin brother had died at birth. Jim Lewis, however, learned at age 6 that he was a twin and that his brother had been adopted by another family. His mother, Lucille Lewis, who has since remarried and now goes by the name of Lucille Cheny, began to encourage him even then to look for his lost brother, but procrastinated. Finally, last January, he went to court and started the proceedings. On February 9, the reunion took place.

When identical twins James Arthur Springer and James Edward Lewis were reunited after spending all but the first four weeks of their 39 years apart, they discovered that, despite the long separation, their lives had been astonishingly similar. Aside from sharing a given name, each married and then divorced a woman named Linda. Their second wives were both named Betty. Springer named his first son James Allan. Lewis named his first son James Allan. Each man grew up with an adopted brother named Larry. During childhood, each owned a dog named Toy. Both twins had law-enforcement training and had worked part time as deputy sheriffs in their Ohio towns 70-miles apart. They shared many common interests, such as mechanical drawing, block lettering and carpentry. Both said their favourite school subject was Maths, their least favorite was spelling. They vacationed at the same time, three-block-long beach near St. Petersburg, Fla., both getting there and back in a Chevrolet. Their smoking and drinking patterns were nearly identical.

The twins were tickled. "This is really blowing our minds," said Springer. " Just unbelievable. It's weird. It's downright spooky." "We even use the same slang," Lewis added. "A lot of times, I'll start to say something, and he'll finish it!" (Researchers said when asked about this phenomenon that identical twins are known to have remarkably similar brain waves, which may contribute to the perception that such twins "think alike"). Doctors and scientists were equally surprised by the findings. "If someone else brought this material to me and said: 'This is what I've got,' I'd say I didn't believe it," said psychologist Thomas J. Bouchard Jr., Director of the Minnesota Study of Twins Reared Apart Project, a team that gathered to look into Springer, Lewis and other twins separated in childhood. "The probability of two people independently being given the same name is not that rare. But when you start to compound the coincidences, they become highly unlikely very quickly. In fact, I'm flabbergasted by some of the similarities."

Even more interesting to researchers about twins like Springer and Lewis, however, is the fact that they are a "living laboratory" in which it is possible to examine closely the relative influence of heredity versus environment on the medical and behavioral aspects of human development.

Nearly 20 other such pairs have come to the attention of the University of Minnesota researchers, and at least eight of them have already been enrolled in the study (others are being courted assiduously for their participation). "It could be the most dense volume of data ever gathered on any group of people," said Bouchard. "The University of Minnesota will literally be the world center for the study of twins reared apart. Jim and Jim were undoubtedly the catalysts."

Among the medically significant findings in the study of Springer and Lewis is a form of headache called "mixed headache syndrome," a tension headache that turns into a migraine. It has long been thought to be without genetic basis, but scientists now postulate that heredity may indeed be a factor in this viselike pain caused by muscle contractions, the most common type of headache.

"Springer and Lewis both have peculiar elements to their headaches," said Dr. Leonard Heston, a member of the Minnesota team. "The syndrome began at age 18 for both; each gets it with the same degree of disability and the same frequency — and they used almost identical words to describe it."

Thus, the reunion of Springer and Lewis comes at a time when global interest in the study of twins has definitely been on the upswing. But identical twins reared apart are thought to be a diminishing occurrence, because of more enlightened welfare policies and changing social mores that have removed much of the social disgrace once associated with illegitimacy. When these twins were born slightly premature on Aug. 19, 1939, at the Piqua, Ohio, Memorial Hospital, however, their mother, an unwed, 35-yearold immigrant, immediately put them up for adoption.

The brothers shook hands stiffly, when they saw each other for the first time. Then they hugged and burst into laughter. "I looked into his eyes and saw a reflection of myself," Springer recalled. "I wanted to scream or cry, but all I could do was laugh."

One of the first such experiments was published in 1965 in the journal 'Science'. That study reported that the EEGs of pairs of separated identical twins (two such pairs out of 15 pairs tested) displayed unexpected correspondences. When one twin was asked to close his or her eyes, which causes the brain's alpha rhythms to increase, the distant twin's alpha rhythms were also found to increase. The same effect was not observed in unrelated pairs of people.

9.7 A True Story of Human-Animal Quantum Entanglement

During the 1920s, a two-year-old dog named Bobbie, mostly collie with a bit of English sheep dog, became a national sensation. His owners, Mr. and Mrs. Frank Brazier, restaurant owners in Silverton, Oregon, were vacationing in Indiana when Bobbie got lost. Despite intense efforts to locate the dog, the Braziers finally despaired of finding him. Broken-hearted, they resumed their trip westward, never expecting to see him again. Six months later Bobbie showed up, emaciated, at the family restaurant in Oregon. He ran upstairs to the second-floor living quarters and jumped on the bed, awakening Frank Brazier by licking his face.

No one could believe it. But when the Silverton Appeal published the story, it quickly spread to newspapers across the country, and hundreds of people sent letters to the Braziers claiming they'd seen Bobbie and were able to confirm his identity by several distinguishing marks. Still dubious, the Oregon Humane Society launched an investigation into the Braziers' claims. By interviewing people who claimed to have seen him, they reconstructed the route home, which they estimated was around 2,800 miles, much of which took place in the dead of winter. Bobbie did not follow his owners' route back to Oregon, but travelled an indirect course over land he had never seen nor could have been familiar with. This was no lookalike dog; his owners were able to identify him not only because of his loving behaviour, but also by several unique marks and scars.

9.8 An Example of my own Family on Quantum Entanglement

Let me share the following thoughts with you.

I have got two children: one son (42 years) and one daughter (40 years). Both are happily settled with their spouses and kids in different cities (son in Austin, USA, and daughter in Bangalore, India) away from our home in Gurgaon (in India) where my wife and I are (happily) staying together. My wife receives at least one call per day from each of our children just to chit-chat and exchange news of the respective families. As such, she may be receiving about 20 calls per day on an average from different people. And there is no fixed time of the day when our children would call their mother. But it so happens that, out of these 20 calls per day, whenever her phone rings at some time, my wife would just rush to pick up that call by telling me (in advance) that it is the call definitely from our son or from our daughter. And it turns out to be so. Why does it happen? It means that our souls are quantumly entangled with those of our children because of which we can sense their calls in advance.

Similarly, if your loved one (son or daughter) has not called you for the last few days, you are thinking about him/her. Suddenly you pick up your mobile phone to call your loved one. But what has happened? A moment before you start dialling his/her number, your phone rings and your loved one is calling you from the other side. Has it happened with you or not? Why do your loved get a premonition that you are remembering him/her so intensely? It is because your souls are quantumly entangled.

Extending this argument to a deeper level, this whole Universe is quantumly entangled with each other: living as well as non-living. Each one of us has been born from the same source, call it big-bang explosion or God, whatever, and hence we are all intimately entangled with each other irrespective of time and space separating us. A photon, which started from a particular star several millions of light years ago and heads towards earth, can be given a command during its flight from another quantumly entangled photon to reach the lab on the planet earth in a particular mode. It is because both these photons were together at one particular place and instant and were entangled with each other.

9.9 Quantum Entanglement and Love

People get entangled with each other when they fall in love, and it can start when they're nowhere near each other, perhaps catching each other's eyes for the first time across a crowded room. And it seems that tiny, subatomic particles — things like electrons or photons — can also get entangled with each other at a great distance, in a way that physicists still don't understand but are already starting to make use of.

It's this really delightful, really strange thing of the phenomenon known as "quantum entanglement." Somehow what happens to one particle can have an impact on what we would expect the second one to do, even if those particles are nowhere near each other.

The experience of falling in love is altogether reminiscent of what in quantum physics is known as entanglement.

In the microscopic realm, once two particles experience a shared state, they are no longer separate entities but exist as one. This remains true even when they are separated by a great distance. The "falling" part of the falling in love process requires a falling away of many individual boundaries as the two people merge significant parts of themselves. The coupling moves the two individuals into an entangled sense of oneness.

All living beings are energy fields manifesting through their physical form. Mere physical attraction to another is based on sensory stimulation, but being in lust is not quite the same as being in love. Falling in love requires that our energies coalesce with one another.

When this occurs, our energy field resonates with our partner's energy field, and our vibrations harmonize with each other's so that two individuals are no longer distinctly separate. This energetic interchange happens simultaneously on physical, emotional, and spiritual levels, and it is what makes falling in love—and staying in love—potentially the most fulfilling experience in life.

Over the course of time, however, many people indicate that although they may still love the other, they no longer feel in love. There's a common belief that as the years pass, falling out of love is natural and to be expected. I'd suggest that it may be ordinary, but that doesn't make it natural. Falling in love and sustaining it requires maintaining a sense of oneness.

In the turmoil that we experience when a relationship becomes adversarial, we need to acknowledge or change something to shift the energy away from separation and back toward entangled wholeness. Making that shift may mean changing our beliefs, our perceptions, or our behaviours or possibly all of these. You might ask yourself, "What is my partner seeing in me that I don't see in myself?"

If you set out to recentre the energy field of the initial romantic entanglement or the caring friendship, you can selflessly try to get in the other's shoes. This is an exercise in empathy. Doing this doesn't mean you are abandoning your position; it simply means loving and validating your partner. If I try to appreciate and care about my upset partner's point of view, I'm invoking a shift of energy.

Connecting empathetically with our partner is the most powerful thing we can do in such troubled moments. It can turn the tide from a competitive, maybe even emotionally and verbally abusive, exchange back into a loving energy field once again entangled with caring. (If you try this approach consistently and with genuine affection, but your partner doesn't reciprocate over time, you might well consider whether the relationship is right for you.)

Another way of shifting the energy of a relationship is to express positive feelings or appreciation for your partner. Once a couple's energy has drifted into separatism and conflict, (called 'decoherence' in quantum entanglement) they may default to unloading critical thoughts and feelings with each other. Negativity then fills the divide they have structured.

The quantum society, you see, is not that much different from ours after all: we are made of quanta and immersed into them... who's influencing who? Is there a serious quantum impact on our society? These are just funny ways to try to relate the microscopic world (in which entanglement has probably nothing to do with love) to the world in which we are used to live. Everybody may imagine the situation which in his fantasy best applies to this strange quantum realm. Entanglement is surely one of the mysterious 'gods' of the Book of Nature as we know it today, and "when it comes to entanglement, we've only just discovered the tip of an iceberg".

9.10 Quantumly Entangled Souls, Entangled Universe, Non-Duality, and Entanglement with Ganesha Consciousness

We have thus seen that the quantum entanglement is a metaphysical-like aspect of quantum mechanics. In simple terms, entanglement maintains that observation of one object can instantaneously influence the behaviour of another object, even at very great distances, and even when there appears to be no physical force existing between the two objects. For example, if we pluck a flower on the planet earth, we are going to disturb the equilibrium on a galaxy, hundreds of millions of light years away from the earth. ***Entanglement is a prime example of the non-local nature of quantum mechanics and is an integral part of the concept of "connectedness" in the universe.*** In principle, any two objects that have ever interacted are forever entangled–the behaviour of one instantaneously influences the other. The meta-physicist would say, "We are all connected in some manner because we originated from the same source" and in doing so, we refer to Individual Consciousness and Universal Consciousness, both being integrally one and indistinguishable. ***This is, what is called, Non-duality or Advaita, or merging of individual souls with the Supreme Soul, that is with Ganesha Consciousness.***

In this quantumly-entangled Universe, we are all one, each one originated from the Supreme consciousness and shall merge into the Supreme consciousness, that is Ganesha Consciousness.

Om Shri Gaṇeshāya Namah!

BIBLIOGRAPHY

Dudeja, Jai Paul. ""Future is not separate from the present or the past: Can temporal nonlocality in Quantum Entanglement explain Retrocausality (effect preceding the cause), Precognition and Déjà vu?", Journal of Emerging Technologies and Innovative Research (JETIR, ISSN: 2349-5162, www.jetir.org), Vol. 6, Issue 5, May 2019, 304-311. http://doi.one/10.1729/Journal.20646

Dudeja, Jai Paul. "Happiness explained by the ancient Hindu Scriptures and the temporal nonlocality in Quantum Entanglement", Journal of Emerging Technologies and Innovative Research (JETIR, ISSN: 2349-5162, www.jetir.org), Vol. 6, Issue 6, June 2019, 531-540. http://doi.one/10.1729/ Journal.21364

Dudeja, Jai Paul. "Quantum Physics of Consciousness and Non-duality in Eastern Philosophy", BlueRose Publishers, 2021.

Dudeja, Jai Paul. "Quantum Science of Love, Healing, Happiness, and Bliss in Ancient Wisdom", Prakhar Goonj Publication, 2021.

Dudeja, Jai Paul. "Spiritual and Scientific Significance of the Number 108", International Journal of Yogic,

Human Movement and Sports Sciences, (ISSN: 2456-4419), Vol. 3, Issue. 1, 2018, pp 611-615.

Krishnananda, Swami. "Commentary on the Panchadasi", Divine Life Society, Rishikesh, India, 1989.

Rajendran, Abhilash. Prof Gregory Baily (Translator); C. Devadas (Ed.). "Ganesha Gita From Ganesha Purana". www.hindu-blog.com, May 2013.

Ramachander, P. R. (Translator), "Ganapati Dhyana Slokas: Dwathimsath Ganapathi Dhyana Slokas".

Rao, V.D. N. "Essence of Ganesha Mahima (Ganesha Purana Saaraamsha Added)", www.kamakoti. org./ books